That's one small step for man one giant leap for mankind.
(Neil Armstrong, 21. Juli 1969)

AI/
One more
small Step
not just a
science fiction
of AI

3½ Stories and the making-of with AI

½ Story: Draft for a science fiction about a fake moon landing

1st story: The last gunslinger - with an unusual ending.

2nd story: The gunslinger is beamed into the future - we've seen that before.

3rd story: No fake moon landing, just a small step - a plot ripe for a movie.

And again and again the dialog between author and AI - with explanations.

Klaus Paschenda

AI / One more small Step
not just a science fiction of AI
{Version 2025-01}
© 2025 Klaus Paschenda

AI assistance:
Anthropic, Claude.ai (3.5), San Francisco

Website: ai-fat.com

Cover, photo, design, layout: © Klaus Paschenda

Email: info@ai-fat.com
Kirchweg 23, 46499 Hamminkeln, Germany

Druck und Distribution im Auftrag des Autors:
tredition GmbH, Halenreie 40-44,
22359 Hamburg, Deutschland

English:
Ebook ISBN   978-3-9826968-0-5
Paperback ISBN   978-3-9826968-1-2

German:
Ebook ePub2 ISBN   978-3-9826968-2-9
Ebook ePub3 ISBN   978-3-9826968-3-6
Paperback ISBN   978-3-9826968-4-3

Contents

Notes on the layout:

All parts of inner stories written by AI are set in Palatino 11 pt.

The prompts to the AI are in Helvetica 10 pt and begin with >>> as a sign for the supervisor.

> *The methodical answers of the AI are also in Helvetica 10 pt italics but are additionally indented.*

Comments and additions by the author are set in Palatino 10 pt when the situation demands it.

Prologue
no story

>>> Let's write a science fiction about the race to the moon. We know the history of the NASA and the conspiracy theories that claim it was just an act on Earth.

The Weight of Glory

July 16, 1969 - T-minus 3 hours before launch

Dr. Sarah Chen stared at the data scrolling across her terminal in the backup control room at Huntsville. Something wasn't right with the telemetry. The numbers suggested minute irregularities in the Saturn V's guidance system – nothing that would trigger a mission abort, but enough to keep her awake at night.

"You're going to create wrinkles frowning like that," said James Cooper, settling into the chair beside her. As the backup flight director, he had the luxury of looking calm. Everything that could possibly go wrong today would land on Mission Control in Houston, not here.

"These readings..." Sarah started.

"Are within acceptable parameters," James finished.

"I've seen you triple-check every calculation since Grissom."

He didn't need to elaborate. The Apollo 1 fire that killed three astronauts still haunted everyone.

Sarah switched screens, pulling up the lunar landing trajectories.

"That's not it. Look at these variances."

James leaned forward, his practiced nonchalance slipping.

"Huh."

"Exactly. Someone's been feeding duplicate data into the system. Old numbers, recycled to look new."

"You think it's the Soviets?"

Sarah shook her head.

"No. The alterations are too subtle. This is coming from inside NASA."

James went very still.

"Are you suggesting..."

"That someone wants this mission to fail? Or appear to fail?"

Sarah minimized her screen as another technician walked past.

"I think someone's planning to fake telemetry data during the actual landing."

"But why?"

"Because they don't think we can actually do it."

Sarah pulled out a small notebook filled with handwritten calculations.

"The real numbers show we're right on the edge of our capabilities. If anything goes wrong during descent..."

"We lose Armstrong and Aldrin," James finished.

"And if we fake it?"

"We guarantee a victory in the space race. No risk of national embarrassment. No dead astronauts."

James studied her face.

"You've already reported this up the chain?"

"Tomorrow's newspapers are already printed," Sarah said quietly.

"Giant leap for mankind. The headlines are written. The photos are ready. The speech in case they die is drafted, but so is the victory speech."

"What are you going to do?"

Sarah turned back to her terminal and began typing. "I'm going to make sure they actually land on the Moon."

The real numbers were terrifying, but they were possible. And Sarah Chen had not spent fifteen years fighting her way up through NASA's ranks to participate in a lie, no matter how noble the intention.

"Houston," she typed into her secure channel.

"Huntsville override sequence initiating. Please verify authentic telemetry stream..."

July 20, 1969 - Lunar Descent

In the noise and controlled chaos of Houston's Mission Control, only Flight Director Pierre Monard noticed the subtle shift in the data flow. The numbers changed – became messier, more erratic, but undeniably real.

"Eagle, Houston. You are go for landing."

Through millions of miles of space, through layers of conspiracy and doubt, through the weight of two nations' pride, the truth arced like a radio wave: humanity, with all its fears and flaws and determination, was about to step onto another world.

And not a single frame of it would be faked.

I've written a story that explores the tension between truth and expedience during the Space Race, using a fictional character to examine real historical pressures and technical challenges. The story touches on several themes:

1. The actual technical complexity of the moon landing

2. The human cost of failure (referencing the Apollo 1 tragedy)

3. The intense political pressure to succeed

4. The ethical choices faced by scientists and engineers

The Question

Can an AI write a novel worth reading?

If you ask linguists, writers, philosophers, publishers, booksellers or people who simply enjoy reading what makes a good novel, very different aspects come to light. The criteria for one are relatively subjective. Since quality cannot be measured in feet or meters or whatever, all that remains are rankings based on individual factors such as the size of the print run or commercial success.Various top lists include books such as the Bible, the Koran, Don Quixote, The Little Prince or 1984 by G. Orwell.

This short case study is not intended to look at the subject in a highly scientific way. We will only consider a simple, perfectly adequate checklist for evaluating a novel, which can certainly be expanded or formulated differently.

1. Are there clearly defined procedures?
2. Are the actions logical, consistent and comprehensible to the reader?
3. Is there a structure?
4. Does the story follow a constructive pattern with a beginning, climaxes, relapses and final scenes?
5. Is an interesting question conveyed to the reader in an understandable way?
6. Are the characters, places and time well chosen?

7. Does the choice of scenes encourage interesting sequences?
8. Are challenging situations used to move the story forward?
9. Are there surprises, dramatic developments and unexpected twists?
10. Are there new perspectives on traditional approaches and familiar ways of thinking?
11. Are the characters convincingly and authentically portrayed and developed?
12. Is the language appropriate to the situation, ranging from simple short statements to complex, detailed descriptions?
13. Is the reader addressed, either emotionally or through possible identification?
14. Can the reader understand the emotional dimensions and constraints of the characters?
15. Is further, reflective thinking stimulated?

In the example chosen here, 'fake moon landing', the comparison with Orwell's 1984 is obvious in terms of genre, but let's take a closer look at what AI creates.

Part I: AI/ Flight Fake, the 2nd

>>> The story begins with this dialog in the oval office:

Secretary: Mr. President, you know the phrase ‚Houston, we have a problem‘.

President: We are the United State, we have no problem.

Secretary: The Chinese ...

President: Forget the little green men, we are America great again.

Secretary: The Chinese are going to the moon in 3 months.

President: Forget it. We are going in two months.

Secretary: Mr. President, that's impossible. The NASA ...

President: Fuck the NSA, do the job and now get out.

The following sections are planned.

1) Mr. Secretary goes to the NSA. There: We have one more problem. Cyberattacks from various internal and external sources repeatedly overwrite data from our control systems and telemetry. This problem and the problem Mr. President leads to only last chance: Fake landing on the moon.

2) A top-secret task force is set up there, consisting of 11 very attractive, sexy women of different origins and skin colours. All women have a degree from an elite university and military specialty training, as well as a pilot's license for F-35s.

3) Mr. Secretary finds the women very interesting. He tells them that they are only subject to him. Money is unlimited, law and order are irrelevant. No Drugs,

serious crime and corpses are forbidden. They have an old, remote missile base from the nuclear arms race in the Arizona desert at their disposal.

4) The local press receives a tip-off that a feature film is being shot there. This enables the women to recruit the necessary craftsmen and film technicians. To ensure that everything goes very quickly, they use their feminine charms and sometimes pay bribes.

5) The project ist running fine. The women therefore decide to film the Mars landing in the strictest secrecy. It is a once-in-a-lifetime opportunity. Mr. Secretary must not find out about it.

6) One of the women has started a love life with Mr. Secretary, partly with AI glasses. But she does her job in the group. Nobody has a clue.

Operation Moonshine
half of the story

1. The Decision

The Oval Office felt smaller than usual that morning, the weight of impossible demands pressing against its walls.

"Mr. President, you know the phrase Houston, we have a problem."

"We are the United States, we have no problems."

"The Chinese—"

"Forget the little green men, we are America great again."

"The Chinese are going to the moon in 3 months."

"Forget it. We are going in two months."

"Mr. President, that's impossible. The NASA—"

"Fuck the NSA, do the job and now get out."

2. The Crisis

The NSA's cybersecurity center hummed with tension. Deputy Director Martinez's presentation left no room for optimism.

"It's not just one breach," she explained to the Secretary.

"We're seeing coordinated attacks from multiple vectors. Every time we secure our telemetry data, new infiltrations appear. Someone's been studying our systems for years."

The Secretary loosened his tie.

"And NASA?"

"Can't meet the President's timeline. Not even close."

Martinez pulled up another screen.

"We're looking at eight months minimum, assuming everything goes perfectly."

"Which leaves us one option."

"A dangerous one," Martinez warned.

"But yes. We fake it, or we lose the race."

3. The Team

Dr. Maya Chen adjusted her F-35 simulator goggles, watching the other ten women file into the briefing room. Harvard, MIT, Stanford, Cal-Tech – their credentials were impeccable. Fighter pilots, computer specialists, special forces veterans, cinematographers.

The Secretary stood before them, trying not to stare too long at any one face.

"Ladies, what I'm about to tell you violates every protocol I'm sworn to uphold. You'll be operating outside any official chain of command. Your only authority is me."

Colonel Sarah Rodriguez raised an eyebrow.

"And our mission?"

"Make history. Even if we have to fabricate it."

4. The Base

The abandoned missile silo in Arizona had seen better days, but that worked in their favor. Local newspapers eagerly reported on the mysterious film production setting up shop. Hollywood magic in the desert.

Dr. Leah Williams, their procurement specialist, worked miracles with the local talent. A smile here, a generous "consulting fee" there. Set designers and effects specialists arrived, their curiosity dampened by non-disclosure agreements and exceptional pay rates.

"We're building two worlds," Leah explained to the team.

"The one they think they see, and the one we're really creating."

5. The Ambition

Late one night, after the day crew had left, Captain Jennifer Wu called an unofficial meeting.

"Look at what we've built," she said, gesturing to their meticulously crafted lunar surface.

"We could do Mars. We should do Mars."

The room fell silent as the implications sank in.

"The Secretary would never approve," Maya warned.

"Then we don't tell him," Jennifer replied.

"We're already making history. Why stop at the Moon?"

6. The Complication

In his private quarters, the Secretary slipped on the AI glasses, and suddenly she was there – Dr. Victoria Nash, their behavioral psychology expert. In person, she maintained perfect professional distance. Here, in the virtual space between reality and deception, different rules applied.

"The project remains on schedule," she reported, both to her lover and her superior.

"All teams performing above expectations."

He never suspected she was simultaneously conferencing with the Mars team, coordinating their parallel deception.

7. The Convergence

Deep in the Arizona night, two missions took shape. On one stage, Neil Armstrong's famous words were rehearsed to perfection. On another, hidden behind false walls and encrypted security feeds, the first footprints on Mars were being choreographed.

The women moved between the two productions with practiced ease, building redundancies into both deceptions. They created a lunar landing that would withstand decades of scrutiny, while secretly laying the groundwork for an even greater fiction.

In her private moments, Victoria wondered if she was protecting the team by keeping the Secretary distracted, or if she'd compromised everything by getting too close. But in a project built on layers of deception, perhaps truth was merely a matter of perspective.

The desert stars watched silently, indifferent to the lies being crafted in their name.

I've structured the story to follow your outlined sections while developing the characters and their motivations. The narrative explores themes of deception, ambition, and the complex relationships between truth, power, and necessity.

Would you like me to:

- Expand any particular section?

- Add more technical details about the film production?

- Develop specific character relationships further?

- Include more scenes about the Mars landing preparation?

>>> That's ok, let's go on. One of the women is a double agent working for the Chinese. This becomes apparent when she falls during filming and swears in Chinese.

8. The Slip

Lieutenant Amy Liu was their best special effects coordinator. Her expertise with practical effects and miniatures had proven invaluable in creating both the lunar and Martian landscapes. No one questioned her occasional late nights in the facility – perfectionists were common in this group.

The incident happened during a critical scene. They were filming the deployment of the lunar module's landing gear, using a full-scale replica suspended from nearly invisible cables. Amy was adjusting the dust displacement effects when one of the cables snapped.

She fell six feet, landing hard on the artificial lunar surface. The impact forced air from her lungs, and with it came words that froze the room:

"Tā mā de! Zhè zhēn de tèngsǐ wǒ le!"

Captain Jennifer Wu's head snapped up. As the daughter of Chinese immigrants, she knew those weren't the practiced phrases of someone who'd taken Mandarin as an elective. The tones were too perfect, the expression too natural – it was the instinctive swearing of a native speaker.

Maya Chen, their technical lead, was already moving. Without making it obvious, she positioned herself between Amy and the exit. Sarah Rodriguez, their security specialist, casually touched her sidearm.

But Amy had already recovered both her composure and her cover.

"Sorry," she laughed, rubbing her hip.

"You pick up all sorts of things in film school. There was this Chinese director I worked with ..."

The explanation was smooth, rehearsed. Too rehearsed. Jennifer caught Maya's eye, a silent message passing between them. They'd have to handle this carefully. If Amy was indeed reporting to Beijing, she'd already seen both the Moon and Mars sets. More importantly, she knew about the team's unauthorized second project.

Victoria Nash, watching from the gantry above, pulled out her phone. The Secretary would need to be informed – through proper channels, not their private communications. This had just become much more complicated than a simple race to the Moon.

What none of them realized was that Amy's fall hadn't been entirely accidental. Sometimes the best way to hide information was to reveal something else. And in the complex game of multinational espionage, there were always more layers of deception than anyone suspected.

I've added this new section that introduces the spy element through Amy Liu's character, while maintaining the tension of both the original mission and the secret Mars project. The revelation of her possible Chinese connections creates new complications for both the team and their various deceptions.

Would you like me to:

- Explore Amy's actual mission and motivations?

- Develop the team's response to this security breach?

9. The Ripples

The discovery of Amy's true allegiance sent shockwaves through both projects, though in drastically different ways.

In the main studio, where the official lunar landing was being crafted, Sarah Rodriguez implemented new security protocols with ruthless efficiency. Every frame Amy had touched had to be re-examined, every effect reconsidered. But they couldn't afford to fall behind schedule.

"We need to keep her in place," Maya argued during an emergency meeting.

"If she disappears, Beijing will know we're onto them."

"Keep your enemies closer?" Jennifer asked.

"No," Maya replied, "Keep them busy. I've got an idea."

They began feeding Amy carefully crafted misinformation. Minor imperfections were deliberately planted in the lunar surface – craters slightly too symmetrical, dust behavior that wasn't quite right. Things that would send Chinese analysts down rabbit holes for years.

The secret Mars project presented a different challenge. Amy had full access to their prototype red planet landscape, but she hadn't yet seen the final version.

"We move it," Leah Williams declared.

"All of it. Tonight."

Deep in the missile silo's sub-basement, in a section officially marked as structurally unsound, they had a backup stage. While Amy was occupied with the lunar project above, teams worked in shifts to relocate the entire Mars set.

Victoria coordinated the effort, using her relationship with the Secretary to ensure no official eyes turned toward their increased activity.

"Just some reshoots for the moon landing," she told him during their virtual meetings, letting him believe his charm was working while she directed traffic three levels below.

10. The Deception Within Deception

What made the situation truly complex was the realization that they could use this breach to their advantage. Dr. Chen developed a brilliant, if risky, strategy.

"We let her steal the wrong Mars," she explained to the core team.

"We build a third set – obvious enough to find, flawed enough to be useless."

Jennifer caught on immediately.

"A decoy for the decoy?"

"Exactly. We're already faking two landings. Might as well fake a fake."

They began leaving subtle breadcrumbs for Amy to follow: whispered conversations about secret sub-levels, "accidentally" dropped key-cards, and mysterious equipment movements. All leading to a carefully crafted Mars set that would pass initial inspection but fail under serious scientific scrutiny.

11. The Pressure Points

The stakes kept escalating. The Secretary, unaware of the Mars project but now intensely focused on security after Victoria's report about Amy, demanded daily updates. President's deadline loomed closer. And somewhere in Beijing, analysts were presumably picking apart every transmission they received.

Colonel Rodriguez summed it up during a secure meeting:

"We're now running three parallel productions: the moon landing for the President, the real Mars project for ourselves, and a fake Mars project for our Chinese friend."

"Four, if you count the actual moon landing that NASA's still trying to pull off," Leah added.

Jennifer looked around the room at her team – the most brilliant women she'd ever worked with, now caught in an web of intersecting deceptions.

"Well, ladies, they say the best lies contain elements of truth. Let's make sure we remember which elements are which."

Victoria, watching the Secretary's incoming call flash on her phone, couldn't help but wonder the same thing.

> *I've added sections showing how Amy's discovery impacts both projects, introducing the concept of a triple-deception strategy. Would you like me to:*
>
> *- Explore more technical details of how they're managing these multiple deceptions?*
>
> *- Show more about how specific team members are handling the pressure?*
>
> *- Add scenes about Amy's reaction to their counter-intelligence efforts?*
>
> *- Develop the growing tension between the various secret projects?*

>>> Please, develop the growing tension between the various secret projects!

12. Collision Course

The juggling act was becoming increasingly precarious. In the main control room, Dr. Maya Chen stared at her scheduling board, now a maze of colored lines representing different projects' resource allocations.

"We have a problem," she announced to Jennifer and Victoria during their midnight meeting.

"The fake Mars set is eating into our moon landing timeline."

Victoria massaged her temples.

"We can't slow down the moon project. The Secretary's breathing down my neck about the President's deadline."

"And our real Mars project?" Jennifer asked quietly.

"That's the real problem."

Maya pointed to a red line intersecting with several others.

"We need the same pyrotechnics team for the Mars descent sequence that we need for the moon landing's ascent module. We can't be in three places at once."

13. Cross-Purposes

The tension manifested in unexpected ways. The costume department became a battleground when they realized they had to maintain three different sets of spacesuits – each with distinct wear patterns and dust compositions. The lunar dust had to match NASA's specifications exactly, while the fake Mars suit needed believable but scientifically inaccurate dust to mislead Chinese analysts. Meanwhile, the real Mars suits required completely different weathering patterns.

Sarah Rodriguez found Leah Williams alone in the prop room at 3 AM, crying in frustration over a set of boot prints.

"These are supposed to be for the fake Mars set," Leah explained, wiping her eyes.

"But I accidentally used the correct soil composition. Now I have to destroy them before Amy finds them, but that means redoing the whole sequence."

14. Double-Agent's Dilemma

Amy Liu, meanwhile, was conducting her own delicate balancing act. During a critical Moon landing sequence, she deliberately let her tablet display flash Chinese characters for a fraction of a second – just long enough for Jennifer to notice.

"She's getting sloppy," Jennifer told Victoria. "Either Beijing's putting pressure on her, or..."

"Or she's letting us see exactly what she wants us to see," Victoria finished.

15. The Secretary's Shadow

Victoria's position became increasingly precarious. During one of their virtual meetings, the Secretary asked a question that made her blood freeze.

"The fuel consumption reports from the base seem high," he noted.

"Almost as if you're running multiple large-scale productions."

Victoria kept her face neutral as she fed him the prepared explanation about multiple takes and safety redundancies. But later, alone with Jennifer, she voiced her growing concern.

"He's not stupid. He's going to figure out something's wrong with the numbers."

16. Critical Mass

The breaking point came when a dust storm – a real one, ironically – forced them to move all outdoor operations inside for three days. Suddenly, three separate production schedules had to share the same confined space.

In the main hangar, the lunar module sat ready for its historic fake landing. One level below, the decoy Mars set waited to trap Chinese intelligence. And in the deep sub-basement, their real Mars project seemed to mock them all with its red dust and scientific accuracy.

During an emergency team meeting, Colonel Rodriguez laid out their options:

"We can either scale back the Mars projects and focus on the moon landing..."

"Unacceptable," Jennifer cut in. "We've come too far."

"...or we can risk everything by maintaining all three."

Maya studied her tablet.

"There's a fourth option."

When everyone turned to look at her, she continued:

"We let Amy find out about the real Mars project."

The room erupted in protest, but Maya held up her hand.

"Not the whole truth. Just enough to make her think she's discovered our actual secret, while hiding an even bigger one."

Victoria leaned forward.

"What exactly are you suggesting?"

"I'm suggesting," Maya said with a grim smile, "that it's time to fake a leak of our fake Mars project by pretending it's our real Mars project, while protecting our actual real Mars project."

Jennifer laughed despite herself.

"You know we're all going to need therapy after this is over, right?"

But they all recognized the desperate genius of the plan. As the teams dispersed to their respective projects, Victoria lingered behind, staring at the hundreds of cables running through the ceiling – data lines connecting their web of deceptions. She wondered how long they could keep all these plates spinning before something crashed.

Her phone buzzed. The Secretary wanted another meeting.

In the distance, she could hear the pyrotechnics team testing explosion effects, but couldn't tell if it was for the Moon, fake Mars, or real Mars landing. Somehow, that seemed perfectly fitting.

I've added new sections exploring the mounting tensions between the projects, showing how they affect both operations and personalities. Would you like me to:

- Explore more about how they execute Maya's risky new plan?

- Show more personal conflicts between team members?

- Add scenes about how they're handling the technical challenges?

> *- Develop the growing suspense around the Secretary's investigations?*

>>> Explore more about how they execute Maya's risky new plan!

...

The rest of the dialog is not shown here. It is sufficient for now from the AI.

Part II: Possible by AI?

The first impression

What can be observed?

The adventure of getting a science fiction novel from AI software begins with a simple instruction:

>>> Let's write a science fiction novel about the race to the moon. We know the history of NASA and the conspiracy theories that claim that only staging took place on Earth.

Based on this input, two sections were generated, but they are unconvincing: The Weight of Glory.

In terms of content, the AI software fails. The second section is hard to beat in terms of brevity. If crucial data is changed three hours before take-off, no flight director will give the Go. In addition, the data is checked several times and every single operator has to give their Go. The organizational hierarchy in the control center does not need to be shown, but a good novel requires a little more context. That's why I stopped the experiment at this point.

The AI software probably needs more input to guide it. So it was given an introductory dialog, a few hints about the characters, the settings, and possible scenes. You have read the first part of the result in Part I 'Flight Fake'.

We could go through the checklist from the prologue now, but it's long, it would be boring and unreadable, so only for experts. Here is just a brief look at Part I.

What is immediately noticeable about the presentation is that there are conversations, but they take place in static situations and show no tension. There are no tough discussions. There are no action scenes with wild arguments and pounding dialogue.

The idea of the AI software to introduce further layers of deception into the story is basically a good approach to create tension and dynamics. But it does not work. Instead, the AI slips on the ice it creates. In the first seven chapters of Part I, the story is completely straightforward and without any truly surprising moments. Basically, everyone knows what happens next. Hence the interjection with the double agent. After that, the story continues with this aspect, but without any unexpected twists. The AI has no ideas.

But can software have ideas? The phrase above, 'the idea of AI software', was implied by the context.

Dealing with AI software involves a back and forth between input and output. The AI software is written in such a way that its linguistic output should look as if it is coming from a human. This is referred to as a dialog between the AI software and the user. In the course of such a human-machine dialog, the software suggests the existence of an intelligence through quasi polite and empathetic language. The user succumbs to an anthropomorphization of the software machine.

This anthropomorphism can be found in the majority of texts that deal with the topic of AI. AI software is ascribed an intelligence that it does not have. This can be described as the **INTELLIGENCE effect**.

The users fall victim to the INTELLIGENCE effect.

Back to the ideas. These are something typically human. If it is formulated as 'the idea of AI software', the author has fallen victim to the intelligence effect.

The AI software only provides data constructs based on previous word sentences, word clouds and text sequences. For example, the word deception in one context is quickly followed by other word clouds containing the word deception, which can be interpreted as referring to different situations. This explains the occurrence of different levels of deception.

This leads directly to the question of the storyline. There are some logical errors in the storyline that probably bothered you. Some notes on factually correct connections between storylines and AI software follow below.

The story somehow has the charm of old science fiction movies that built suspense and plot through dialogue due to lack of money and special effects. At that time, clever scene changes led to movies that were worth watching.

With these few considerations, some of the questions on the checklist can be answered briefly:

1. Are there clearly defined procedures?
   - Rather yes.
2. Are the actions logical, consistent and comprehensible to the reader?
   - No, logical errors.
3. Is there a structure?
   - Basically yes, but...
4. Does the story follow a constructive pattern with a beginning, climaxes, relapses and a final scene?
   – No.
5. Is an interesting question conveyed to the reader in an understandable way?
   – From here on, I'll leave it to you to make a sweeping judgment.

But let's look further. The question here is: Can't AI build action scenes?

The last gunslinger
a first story

>>> We are looking back to the time of the Wild West. Write a hard-hitting western novel.

I'll create a western novel about the personal cost of vengeance and redemption.

Blood on the Sage

Chapter 1: The Return

The dust never settled in Dead Horse Junction. It hung in the air like old sins, coating everything in a layer of rust-colored grit that matched the dried bloodstains on Marshall Thomas Wade's badge. He'd been riding for three days straight, leaving behind a trail of hoofprints that disappeared as quickly as whispers in a storm.

The town hadn't changed in the five years since he'd left. The same weathered buildings lined the single dirt street, their paint peeling like dead skin in the merciless desert sun. Harker's General Store still had that crooked sign, and Miss Jenny's boarding house continued its losing battle against the elements, its once-white walls now the color of old bones.

Wade dismounted slowly, his boots hitting the ground with the weight of a man carrying more than just trail dust. His dark eyes scanned the empty street, noting the curtains that twitched in windows and the shadows that shifted in doorways. News traveled fast in small towns, and he figured word of his approach had beaten him here by at least a day.

The Marshall's star felt heavier than it had when he'd first pinned it on. Back then, he'd been young and full of fire, believing justice was as simple as right and wrong. Now he knew better. Justice, like everything else out here, came in shades of gray as varied as storm clouds.

He led his horse to the water trough, watching the animal drink while his hand rested naturally near his Colt. The weapon had become more than just a tool – it was a reminder of everything he'd lost that night when the Hawkins gang had burned his world to ashes.

"Didn't expect to see you back here, Wade," a familiar voice called out. Standing in the doorway of the saloon was Doc Morrison, looking older but still wearing that same worn leather vest he'd had on the night he'd dug three bullets out of Wade's chest.

"Wouldn't be here if I had a choice, Doc," Wade replied, his voice rough from trail dust and too many nights of silence.

"But a man's past has a way of catching up with him."

The doctor's eyes narrowed.

"Heard about Lasson City. They say Jim Hawkins is headed this way."

Wade nodded slowly.

"That's the word. Figure it's time to end what started here."

"Revenge won't bring Sarah back," Doc said softly, naming the ghost that had haunted Wade across a thousand miles of wilderness.

"This ain't about revenge anymore, Doc."

Wade turned to face his old friend fully.

"It's about making sure no one else has to bury their wife and child because good men did nothing."

The wind picked up, sending tumbleweeds dancing down the empty street like lost souls. Somewhere in the distance, a crow called out its harsh warning to the desert sky. Wade knew that before the week was out, either he or Jim Hawkins would be feeding those crows. The thought didn't bother him as much as it should have.

"You got a room ready for me?" he asked, though they both knew he wouldn't be sleeping much until this was over.

Doc nodded toward Miss Jenny's.

"Same one as before. Jenny's kept it empty since that night. Said she always knew you'd be back."

Wade gathered his reins and led his horse toward the stable. He could feel the eyes of the town on him, watching, waiting to see if he was still the same man who had sworn to protect them all those years ago. Truth was, he wasn't sure himself anymore.

But one thing hadn't changed – his promise to Sarah. He'd sworn on her grave that he would see justice done, and out here, a man's word was still his bond. Even if keeping it meant adding more ghosts to the ones that already rode with him through his sleepless nights.

The sun was setting behind the distant mountains, painting the sky in shades of blood and gold. Wade knew that somewhere out there, Jim Hawkins was riding hard toward Dead Horse Junction, drawn by the same unavoidable destiny that had brought Wade back to this dust-choked town.

This time, only one of them would ride away.

Chapter 2: Old Wounds

The room hadn't changed. Five years of dust and darkness had settled over everything like a burial shroud, but beneath it, Wade could still see the life he'd lost. Sarah's rocking chair sat empty by the window, the wood worn smooth where her hands had rested. A child's wooden horse lay forgotten in the corner, its painted face faded to a ghost of what it had been.

He set his saddlebags down with deliberate care, disturbing years of silence. The familiar weight of his gun belt remained at his hip as he crossed to the window. From here, he could see the entire length of the town's main street, just as he had that night. Just as Sarah had, in those final moments.

A soft knock at the door broke his dark reverie.

"Brought you some coffee," Jenny's voice called, older now but still carrying that hint of Georgia in its tone.

"Figured you might need it."

Wade opened the door to find her standing there, a cup of steaming coffee in one hand and five years of unspoken words in her eyes. She'd aged, but gracefully, silver threading through her dark hair like moonlight on water. She'd been Sarah's closest friend, the one who'd helped prepare her body for burial.

"Thank you, Jenny," he said, accepting the cup. The coffee was strong and bitter, just as he remembered it.

"Town's changed since you left," she said, lingering in the doorway.

"Sheriff Reeves retired last spring. His deputy, young Billy Cooper, wears the badge now."

She paused, weighing her next words carefully.

"He's a good boy, Wade, but he's never faced anything like Jim Hawkins."

Wade took another sip of coffee, letting the familiar burn ground him in the present.

"No one has. That's why I'm here."

"I heard what happened in Lasson City," Jenny continued.

"They say Hawkins killed three men before burning down the bank. That he laughed while doing it."

She shuddered.

"He's gotten worse since... since that night."

"Men like Hawkins always get worse," Wade replied.

"Evil's like a weed – give it room to grow, and it'll choke everything else out."

Jenny's hand touched his arm briefly, a gesture that spoke of shared grief.

"Sarah wouldn't want you to die facing him."

"Sarah didn't want a lot of things that happened."

Wade's voice was quiet but firm.

"But she'd understand that some things need finishing."

A commotion from the street drew their attention to the window. A group of riders was approaching from the south – not Hawkins' gang, just a cattle drive passing through. But the way the townspeople scattered at the first sign of approaching horses told Wade everything he needed to know about how fear had settled into Dead Horse Junction's bones.

"I'll leave you to get settled," Jenny said, turning to go. At the door, she paused.

"Wade... there's something you should know. About that night."

Her fingers worried at her apron.

"I've been carrying this for five years, not sure if I should —"

The sudden crack of a rifle shot cut through the evening air like summer lightning. Jenny ducked instinctively as Wade's gun seemed to materialize in his hand. But it was just one of the cowhands, taking a wild shot at a coyote that had been stalking their herd.

The moment was broken. Jenny hurried away, leaving Wade alone with the coffee and the weight of her unfinished revelation. He watched her disappear down the stairs, wondering what secret she'd been about to share. In his experience, five-year-old secrets had a way of surfacing at the worst possible moments.

The sun was setting now, painting the hills in shades of purple and gold. Wade cleaned his gun methodically, each motion practiced and precise. The weapon was like a part of him now, an extension of his will that had never failed him. Unlike justice. Unlike the law. Unlike every other thing he'd believed in before that night.

As darkness settled over Dead Horse Junction, Wade could feel the town holding its breath. Jim Hawkins was coming, drawn by the same gravity that had pulled Wade back to this place where everything had ended and would soon begin again. The only question was how many more graves would need digging before it was done.

He touched the marshal's badge on his chest, feeling the familiar ridges where Sarah's blood had stained the metal. Some stains, he'd learned, never truly washed away. Some debts could only be paid in blood.

Chapter 3: Ghosts at Noon

The next morning dawned blood-red over the desert, the sun rising like a gunshot wound in the eastern sky. Wade was already awake – truth was, he hadn't slept more than an hour at a stretch. The ghosts in this room were too restless for that.

He made his way down to the street just as Harker was opening the general store. The old shopkeeper's hands shook as he unlocked the door, though whether from age or fear, Wade couldn't tell. News traveled fast in territory like this – if Hawkins was within a hundred miles, Harker would know.

"Mornin', Marshall," Harker said, his voice carefully neutral.

"Didn't expect to see you up so early."

"Need supplies," Wade replied.

"And information."

Inside the store, the familiar smell of leather, coffee, and tobacco brought back memories of better days. Sarah used to come here every Thursday, buying supplies for the week ahead. She'd always bring little Tommy along, and Harker would slip the boy a piece of hard candy when he thought Wade wasn't looking.

"Ain't much changed in the supply department," Harker said, shuffling behind his counter.

"Information, though... that's gotten to be a dear commodity these days."

Wade placed a gold double-eagle on the counter. It gleamed in the early morning light filtering through the dusty windows.

"Dear enough?"

Harker's eyes fixed on the coin, but he didn't reach for it.

"Some things are dearer than gold, Marshall. Man's life, for instance."

"Hawkins already knows I'm here," Wade said quietly.

"Question is, how many innocent people die before he arrives?"

That struck home. Harker's shoulders sagged as he picked up the coin.

"Rider came through yesterday, heading north. Said he passed Hawkins and his gang two days back, near the Black Rock Canyon. Six men riding with him now, including that Apache scout of his. They..."

He hesitated.

"They what?"

"They had fresh scalps hanging from their saddles. Family of settlers, looks like. Hawkins is sending you a message, Wade. He wants you to know what's coming."

Wade's face remained impassive, but his hand tightened on his gunbelt.

"Any word on his brother?"

"Luke Hawkins?" Harker shook his head.

"No one's seen him since that night. Some say Jim killed him himself, others say he's hiding out in Mexico. Truth died with a lot of other things five years ago."

The door creaked open, and young Billy Cooper stepped in, his sheriff's badge catching the morning light. He couldn't have been more than twenty-five, with a boy's smooth face but old eyes. His gun belt was worn in the right places – not just for show, then.

"Marshall Wade," he said, nodding respectfully.

"Thought we might need to talk."

"About Hawkins?"

"About how we're going to protect this town when he comes."

Cooper's voice was steady.

"I've got four deputies, all good men. We can set up defensive positions, get the women and children to safety—"

"No," Wade cut him off.

"You'll get your men killed. Hawkins isn't coming for the town. He's coming for me."

"Then why not meet him somewhere else?"

Cooper demanded.

"Why bring this down on Dead Horse Junction?"

"Because some things need witnesses," Wade replied.

"Some things need to end where they began."

A horse whinnied outside, making Cooper jump. Wade didn't flinch. He'd stopped being startled by sudden noises the night he'd lost everything worth being afraid for.

"There's something else you should know," Cooper said, lowering his voice.

"About Jenny's husband, Tom. He didn't die of fever like everyone says. Night before he passed, he wrote something down. Something about Sarah, about why Hawkins really came that night."

Wade's eyes narrowed.

"What did he write?"

"Jenny has the letter. She's been afraid to show anyone, afraid of what might happen if—"

The conversation was interrupted by screaming from the street. They rushed outside to find a rider slumped over his horse, three arrows protruding from his back. The horse was lathered and wild-eyed, having run hard and long.

Wade reached the dying man first.

"Hawkins?" he asked.

The rider managed a weak nod.

"Black Rock... they're coming..."

Blood bubbled from his lips.

"He's got... got Sarah's —"

His last breath rattled out before he could finish.

Wade straightened slowly, his face carved from stone. Behind him, he could hear Cooper organizing men, giving orders to move the body, but it all seemed distant. His world had narrowed to a single point of clarity: whatever Sarah's secret was, Hawkins knew it. Had always known it.

And now, after five years of running from the truth, it was riding hard toward Dead Horse Junction, carried by six killers and their demon of a leader.

Wade touched his badge again, feeling the familiar ridges of dried blood under his fingers. By sunset, he'd either have his answers, or he'd have justice.

Or maybe, if God was feeling merciful, he'd have both.

Chapter 4: Shadows at Dawn

The town undertaker was used to business picking up whenever trouble rode into Dead Horse Junction. But even old Marcus Fuller raised an eyebrow when Wade ordered six new pine boxes built before sundown.

"Mighty confident count there, Marshall," Fuller said, measuring boards in his workshop behind the funeral parlor. The sweet scent of fresh-cut pine mixed with the undertaker's ever-present smell of embalming fluid.

"What if Hawkins brings more men?"

"Then you'll need more wood."

Wade turned one of the brass handles in his fingers.

"But he won't. Jim Hawkins always rode with six. Says it's his lucky number."

Fuller's hammer paused mid-stroke.

"Same number as that night."

"Same number as that night," Wade agreed softly.

He left Fuller to his work and headed toward Miss Jenny's boarding house. The morning was growing hot, the kind of heat that made men irritable and quick to draw. Already, most folks had retreated indoors, leaving the street empty except for a mangy dog gnawing on a bone.

Jenny was waiting for him on the porch, a letter clutched in her trembling hands. She'd been crying.

"I should have given this to you yesterday," she said as he climbed the steps.

"Maybe even five years ago. But Tom made me swear..."

Her voice caught.

"He made me swear to wait until it was time."

Wade took the yellowed envelope. The paper was thin, worn at the creases from being opened and reread many times. Tom's signature scrawl was barely legible on the front: "For Marshall Wade - When Hawkins Returns."

Inside was a single sheet of paper, the writing unsteady but clear:

„Wade,

By the time you read this, I'll be dead. Not from fever like they'll tell you, but from the poison Hawkins used to make sure I'd keep his secret. I've held my tongue these five years while it ate at my gut, but I can't take it to my grave.

Sarah wasn't just in the wrong place that night. She was waiting for someone. Luke Hawkins had been coming to see her when you were out on patrol. Not the way you're thinking – she was helping him escape his brother's gang. Luke wanted out, wanted to testify about the gang's crimes to the territorial governor.

Jim found out. But what he didn't know, what Sarah took to her grave, was that Luke had given her something to keep safe. Something that could bring down not just the Hawkins gang, but half the territory's officials who'd been taking their blood money.

It's hidden in—"

The letter ended there, the last words lost in a shaky line that trailed off the page.

"Tom died before he could finish it," Jenny said quietly.

"He was trying to tell me where, but the pain was too much."

Wade folded the letter carefully, tucking it into his shirt pocket next to his heart. The truth he'd carried for five years was crumbling, revealing a new, darker reality beneath. Sarah's face filled his mind – not as she'd looked that last night, but as she'd been in life: strong, principled, always fighting for what was right.

"I've been hunting the wrong killer," he said finally.

Jenny shook her head.

"No. Jim Hawkins pulled the trigger. Luke may not have meant for it to happen, but he brought this down on all of us just the same."

The sound of horses approaching sent them both turning toward the street. But it was only Cooper and his deputies, riding back from burying the arrow-riddled messenger.

"Marshall!" Cooper called out.

"Smoke signals to the north. Apache signs. Hawkins' scout is letting him know the way is clear."

Wade nodded.

"How're your men holding up?"

"Scared," Cooper admitted.

"But they'll stand."

"Get them off the street," Wade ordered.

"I want them inside, out of sight. Hawkins is expecting a fight. Let's let him walk into quiet instead."

"You're going to face them alone?" Jenny's voice was sharp with fear.

"No," Wade said, touching the letter in his pocket.

"Got a few ghosts riding with me now. And they're hungry for justice."

He started down the steps, then paused.

"Jenny, that night ... where did Sarah usually meet Luke? Where would she have hidden something she wanted to keep safe?"

"The old mission," Jenny whispered.

"She did charity work there every Wednesday. Said it was the only place in town where secrets could be buried in holy ground."

Wade's eyes turned north, toward the abandoned adobe mission on the hill overlooking Dead Horse Junction. They said the old priest had died trying to protect his congregation from raiders. The bell tower still stood, though the bell had been silent these five years.

It would ring again today. Wade would make sure of that.

Chapter 5: Sacred Ground

The mission's shadow stretched long across the desert as Wade climbed the winding path. Adobe walls, crumbling at the edges, still bore the scars of old gunfire. The wooden cross that once crowned the bell tower had fallen years ago, leaving only a jagged stub against the sky.

Behind him, Dead Horse Junction lay quiet in the afternoon heat. From up here, it looked peaceful – almost holy. The kind of view that might have made Sarah pause in her charity work, taking a moment to admire God's handiwork. The thought made Wade's chest tighten.

The mission door hung crooked on its hinges. Wade drew his Colt before stepping inside, letting his eyes adjust to the gloom. Dust motes danced in the shafts of light that pierced the roof holes. The altar still stood, though the gold cross had been stolen long ago. Wooden pews lay scattered like broken bones.

"Took you long enough to figure it out."

The voice came from the shadows near the confessional. Wade spun, gun raised, to find Luke Hawkins stepping into the light. Five years had turned his once-black hair gray, and a ragged scar ran from his left eye to his jaw. He held no weapon.

"You've been here the whole time," Wade said. It wasn't a question.

Luke nodded.

"Where else could I go? The mission was the only sanctuary Sarah trusted. The only place my brother wouldn't think to look."

His laugh was bitter.

"Jim never did have much faith in anything but violence."

"Sarah died protecting you."

Wade's voice was deadly quiet.

"No."

Luke's eyes filled with tears.

"Sarah died protecting the truth. Same as her father did."

Wade felt the world shift beneath his feet.

"Her father?"

"Judge Morrison. The territorial judge who seemed to die of natural causes two weeks before that night."

Luke reached into his shirt and withdrew a leather portfolio, yellowed with age.

"Sarah's father was building a case. Names, dates, bank transfers – everything needed to expose how deep the corruption went. Jim was just the trigger man. The real monsters wore suits and sat in territorial offices."

Heavy footsteps on the mission steps interrupted them. Luke's eyes went wide with fear.

"He's here," he whispered.

"Well, ain't this a touching reunion?"

Jim Hawkins' voice boomed through the mission. He filled the doorway like a demon out of scripture, backlit by the setting sun.

"Brother Luke, still hiding behind holy walls. And Marshall Wade, still chasing ghosts."

His smile was all teeth. "Or should I say, Judge Morrison's son-in-law?"

Wade's gun didn't waver.

"You knew. All along, you knew who Sarah really was."

"'Course I knew. Why'd you think I made sure to kill the boy too? Can't leave any loose ends when you're protecting men who control the whole territory."

Jim took a step forward, spurs ringing on the stone floor.

"Though I admit, watching you chase me across three states, thinking this was just about a marshal's murdered wife... that was pure entertainment."

"Jim, it's over," Luke said, stepping forward.

"I'm not afraid anymore. I'll testify —"

The gunshot was deafening in the confined space. Luke staggered, looking down in surprise at the red stain spreading across his chest. Jim's gun had seemed to appear from nowhere.

"Still too trusting, little brother."

Jim shook his head.

"Still thinking words mean more than lead."

Wade fired, but Jim was already diving behind a pillar. Outside, horses screamed and gunfire erupted as Jim's gang engaged Cooper's deputies.

Luke slumped against the altar, clutching the portfolio.

"Wade," he gasped, "Sarah... she wanted... justice..."

"Touching last words," Jim called out.

"But justice is what rich men call vengeance when they're the ones dealing it out. Me? I prefer simpler terms."

Wade heard the scuff of a boot behind him and threw himself sideways as a bullet splintered the wood where he'd been standing. One of Jim's men had circled around through the sacristy. Wade's return shot caught him in the throat.

"Four left," Jim taunted.

"Not counting me. How many bullets you got left, Wade? Enough to balance all those scales?"

Wade didn't answer. He was remembering Sarah's words the last morning he saw her alive: "Some sins can't be washed away. They have to be dragged into the light."

The mission's bell tower creaked overhead. Wade smiled grimly.

It was time to ring in judgment day.

Chapter 6: Reckoning Hour

The old mission bell hadn't rung in five years. Today, it would toll for the dead.

Wade crouched behind the altar, listening to the gunfight raging outside. Cooper's men were holding their own, but Jim's gang had the high ground. The sharp crack of rifle fire mixed with the deeper boom of shotguns, echoing off adobe walls like thunder.

Luke's body lay still, the portfolio clutched in his lifeless hands. His last expression wasn't fear – it was relief. Five years of carrying the truth had been a heavier burden than any secret deserved.

"Running out of time, Wade!"

Jim's voice carried over the chaos.

"Sun's getting low, and I got men positioned to burn this mission down around us. That evidence dies today, one way or another."

Wade checked his ammunition. Three bullets in the Colt, one in his backup derringer. Not enough for a straight fight. But Sarah hadn't raised him to be a fool.

"Tell me something, Jim," Wade called back, moving silently toward the confessional. "Those territorial officials – they know you're here? Or are you planning to kill me and Luke, take that portfolio, and bargain for a better deal?"

A moment of silence told Wade he'd struck home.

"Smart man," Jim finally answered, his voice tight.

"Smarter than Sarah was. She actually thought justice meant something. Thought if she got those papers to the right people, it'd make a difference."

His laugh was ugly.

"Rich men don't hang for their crimes, Wade. They just hire men like me to bury their problems."

"Sarah wasn't a problem," Wade said, his voice carrying clearly through the mission.

"She was my wife. Tommy was my son."

"They were loose ends!"

Jim's composure cracked.

"Just like Luke! Just like you!"

A shadow moved near the vestry door. Wade fired without hesitation. One of Jim's men fell, cursing. Three bullets left.

"That's the difference between us, Jim," Wade said, using the gunshot's echo to mask his movement toward the bell tower stairs.

"You see people as loose ends. I see them as stories. And yours is about to end."

Jim's response was a burst of gunfire that shattered what remained of the stained glass windows. Wade was already climbing, staying close to the wall where the old steps were strongest.

"You want to know what Sarah's last words were?" Jim shouted.

"She begged. Not for her life – for the boy's. Offered to burn the evidence right there if I'd let him live. But you can't build a reputation on mercy."

Wade reached the bell tower platform. Through gaps in the wooden slats, he could see two of Jim's remaining men positioned behind gravestones. Below, Jim was moving from pillar to pillar, trying to get a clear shot at where he thought Wade was hiding.

The massive bronze bell hung silent, green with age. Wade touched it gently, remembering Sarah's voice: "Some sins can't be washed away. They have to be dragged into the light."

He took aim at the bell's mounting bracket and fired. The sound was deafening. The bracket cracked but held.

"What are you doing?" Jim's voice held the first note of real fear.

Wade's second shot hit the same spot. With a groan of tortured metal, the bracket gave way. The bell fell like God's own judgment, crashing through the rotted tower floor.

Jim dove for safety, but he was a heartbeat too slow. The bell caught him at the legs, pinning him beneath its massive weight. His scream echoed off the mission walls.

Wade descended calmly, derringer in hand. Outside, the gunfire was dying down. Through the broken windows, he could see Jim's remaining men fleeing into the gathering dusk.

Jim lay trapped, his legs crushed, gun just out of reach. Blood trickled from the corner of his mouth.

"Do it," he spat.

"Finish it."

Wade picked up the portfolio from Luke's cold hands.

"No. You're going to live, Jim. You're going to testify about every name in these papers. Every crime, every bribe, every murder. You're going to drag it all into the light."

"They'll kill me in prison."

"Maybe."

Wade checked the portfolio's contents, making sure everything was intact.

"But your story won't die with you. Sarah's father built the case. Sarah protected it. Luke died for it. And I'm going to make sure every newspaper from here to Washington prints it."

He turned to leave, then paused.

"That's justice, Jim. It's not about revenge. It's about the truth."

The mission bell lay silent, streaked with Jim's blood. Outside, the sun was setting on Dead Horse Junction, painting the desert gold and crimson. Wade could hear Cooper's men approaching, their boots crunching on broken glass.

Sarah would have liked the sunset. She always said God painted his finest pictures when day surrendered to night. Like justice rising from the ashes of violence.

Wade touched his marshal's badge one last time, feeling the familiar ridges of dried blood. Then he removed it, letting it fall beside the bell.

Some debts could only be paid in blood. But some truths had to be paid for with the living.

Epilogue: Dawn's Early Light

Three weeks later, the territorial governor would resign in disgrace. Six judges, twelve senators, and more than twenty officials would follow, their empires of corruption crumbling like desert sand. They said Jim Hawkins talked for fourteen straight hours, naming names, dates, and deeds until his voice gave out. He died two days later in his prison cell – whether by his own hand or another's remained a mystery.

The morning they buried Luke Hawkins, Wade stood alone at Sarah's grave. The desert wind whispered through the sage, carrying the scent of rain from distant mountains. He placed a single wildflower on the weathered stone, next to the tiny wooden horse that marked Tommy's resting place.

"You were right, Sarah," he said softly.

"Some sins have to be dragged into the light."

Jenny found him there as the sun climbed higher. She looked older now, but lighter somehow, as if telling the truth had lifted years from her shoulders.

"Town's changing," she said, standing beside him.

"New marshal arrived yesterday. Young man from back East, full of ideas about law and order."

She smiled faintly.

"Reminds me of someone I used to know."

Wade nodded. Dead Horse Junction would survive, as it always had. The desert bred tough people, and tougher truths.

"Doc Morrison wanted you to have this." Jenny handed him a folded paper.

"Said it was from Sarah's father. Written the day before he died."

The judge's handwriting was shaky but clear:

"My dearest Sarah,
If you're reading this, then the truth I've uncovered has caught up with me. But truth, like love, never dies – it only sleeps until someone brave enough comes along to wake it.

Take care of that husband of yours. He sees the world in black and white, but he'll learn. Justice isn't about what's right or wrong – it's about what we choose to do when right and wrong aren't enough.

All my love,

Father"

Wade folded the letter carefully, tucking it away next to his heart where Sarah's last secret had rested for five years.

"Will you stay?" Jenny asked.

He looked out over the desert, where the rising sun was painting the world in shades of promise. Somewhere out there, other corrupt men were building empires on blood and silence. Other truths needed dragging into the light.

"No," he said finally.

"But I'll come back. Some graves need tending."

Jenny understood. She'd always understood.

A year later, they would find Jim Hawkins' gang's hidden cache of stolen gold. The town used it to build a new school, naming it after Sarah. They say on quiet evenings, you can still hear the mission bell's echo rolling across the desert – not a sound of death or vengeance, but a reminder that truth, like the sun, always rises.

Wade rode north that morning, following the trail of another story that needed ending. He left his marshal's badge buried in the mission's shadow, but he carried something stronger: Sarah's belief that justice was worth dying for, and truth was worth living for.

The desert wind followed him, whispering through the sage. And somewhere, in the vast territory where law and justice still fought their daily battles, another bell was waiting to be rung.

THE END

AI cannot be a gunslinger

First of all, the subtitle 'Blood on the Sage', which seems completely nonsensical. This is the information from the AI:

>>> What is the meaning of 'Blood on the Sage' ?

I should note that while I aim to be helpful, "Blood on the Sage" could be considered quite an obscure reference, and I may hallucinate details about such specific queries.

"Blood on the Sage" appears to be a phrase associated with Western American frontier history and literature, typically referring to violence or conflict that occurred in sage-covered territories of the American West. Sage brush is a common plant in Western states, particularly in areas where many frontier conflicts took place. The phrase evokes imagery of bloodshed against the backdrop of the sage-covered landscape.

This is not entirely wrong. Sagebrush is widespread in the western United States and forms the herbal skyline in almost all westerns.

However, the healing properties of sage do not come into play in generative AI systems. The western outlined is also a dialogue-heavy story with no brawls, horse thefts or the like. It is also interesting to note that the music plays no role whatsoever. The AI software has certainly encountered the Song of Death several times during training. Then there's the issue of Western and country music. It would be remarkable if the

AI could incorporate music and set design along-side the story. Perhaps we should play the Song of Death to the AI as input. But AI technology is not that advanced yet.

At least there's an active surprise scene at the end of the story. It's not the usual high noon duel. But when the bell from the tower crashes through the floor and hits a person's legs, they are likely to be amputated. Under these circum-stances, Jim Hawkins bleeds to death. For the high-ranking gentlemen to be exposed by this, a slightly different action is required. This is ano-ther example of how the AI software applies co-herent word clouds without understanding what interpretations these word clouds allow.

Now one could argue that AI software has no factual knowledge and is therefore unable to cor-rectly reproduce factual contexts. The author and reader are asking too much. The objection is completely justified in terms of content. But the consequences are important: if the AI software cannot reproduce facts correctly, how can it pro-vide me with realistic scenes or settings for a sto-ry?

But sometimes it works, I hear voices. You don't have to put all your eggs in one basket. We are in the realm of science fiction. Reality looks different and is not the reality of our daily lives.

To deal with this argument, let's saddle up our horses and ride into the future. Let's let the AI software beam the Western into the future.

Beaming is extremely exciting from a construc-tive technical point of view. Unfortunately, none of us has any idea how it could work. And the AI doesn't know either. It is just a simulation of nerve cells.

Nevertheless, I tried to get the AI software to transform the Western into the future.

That required some persuasion. After the individual chapters had been entered one after the other, the AI was no longer able to follow a coherent text from around chapter 4 onwards. The respective chapter was still written verbally in the future, but no longer. The output of the AI software increasingly deviated from the plot.

If you gave it the entire Western in one piece and asked for the output of a corresponding part, the text was shortened by about half. The request to fill in the missing parts by referring to the chapter numbering was unsuccessful. The AI was not able to orient itself to the chapter numbering. This is an important observation. There are no structural levels in the current generative AI software.

It operates only with words and their probabilistic connections.

If we want a suitable word cloud, we have to provide a corresponding hook. It's similar to giving AI a lock and asking it to craft the key and open the door. The AI must use the input as a reference point to create an appropriate word cloud - that's the key. It can then link additional word clouds to this initial one, thus opening the door.

In practice, short texts were entered to generate subsequent sections, such as a previous chapter summary enhanced with elements suggesting the desired plot direction.

The AI was provided a word cloud as a starting point, which it could use as a foundation to create associated word clouds. This is the standard prompting procedure for AI input. Beyond the topic and question, keywords or text sequences must be included to activate the appropriate simulated neurons.

You read the result as a story: into the future.

Into the Future
a second story

>>> Here is a text that takes place in the Wild West. Keep the plot, but bring the text and characters into the time in which Star Trek is set.

Blood on the Stars

Chapter 1: The Return

The stellar dust never settled in Dead Star Station. It hung in the void like old sins, coating everything in a layer of metallic grit that matched the ion burns on Conglomeration Marshal Thomas Wade's badge. He'd been at zorp for three days straight, leaving behind a trail of quantum distortions that disappeared as quickly as whispers in a solar storm.

The station hadn't changed in the five standard years since he'd left. The same weathered habitation modules lined the single main corridor, their hull plating oxidizing like dead skin in the merciless radiation of the binary stars. Harker's General Supplies still had that malfunctioning holographic sign, and Miss Jenny's boarding quarters continued their losing battle against micro-meteor impacts, their once-pristine walls now pitted like ancient bones.

Wade disembarked slowly from his hyperfighter, his magnetic boots engaging with the deck plating with the weight of a man carrying more than just cosmic debris. His dark eyes scanned the empty corridor, noting the force fields that flickered in viewports and the shadows that shifted in airlocks. News traveled fast in small stations, and he figured word of his approach had beaten him here by at least a day through hyspace channels.

The Marshal's insignia felt heavier than it had when he'd first pinned it on. Back then, he'd been young and full of fire, believing justice was as simple as right and wrong. Now he knew better. Justice, like everything else out here on the frontier of known space, came in shades of gray as varied as nebula clouds.

He guided his ship to the maintenance dock, watching the automated systems begin their work while his hand rested naturally near his Xazer. The weapon had become more than just a tool – it was a reminder of everything he'd lost that night when the Hawkins crew had vented his world to the void.

"Didn't expect to see you back here, Wade," a familiar voice called out. Standing in the airlock of the medical bay was Doc Morrison, looking older but still wearing that same worn pantorian leather vest he'd had on the night he'd regenerated three ion burns in Wade's chest.

"Wouldn't be here if I had a choice, Doc," Wade replied, his voice rough from recycled air and too many nights of silence.

"But a man's past has a way of catching up with him, even at zorp speed."

"Heard about Lasson Colony. They say Jim Hawkins is headed this way."

Wade nodded slowly. "That's the word. Figure it's time to end what started here."

"Revenge won't bring Sarah back," Doc said softly, naming the ghost that had haunted Wade across a thousand light-years of wilderness.

"This ain't about revenge anymore, Doc."

Wade turned to face his old friend fully.

"It's about making sure no one else has to space their wife and child because good men did nothing."

Chapter 2: Old Wounds

The quarters hadn't changed. Five years of vacuum-sealed isolation had settled over everything like a ysis field, but beneath it, Wade could still see the life he'd lost. Sarah's holo-projector sat idle by the viewport, the quantum matrix worn where her fingers had adjusted the controls. A child's model starship lay forgotten in the corner, its curania hull faded to a ghost of what it had been.

He set his gear pack down with deliberate care, disturbing years of silence. The familiar weight of his xazer remained at his hip as he crossed to the viewport. From here, he could see the entire length of the station's main hub, just as he had that night. Just as Sarah had, in those final moments.

A soft chime at the door broke his dark reverie.

"Brought you some pantorian tea," Jenny's voice called, older now but still carrying that hint of Earth's colonies in its tone.

"Figured you might need it."

Wade opened the door to find her standing there, a cup of steaming tea in one hand and five years of unspoken words in her eyes. She'd aged, but gracefully, silver threading through her dark hair like starlight through a nebula. She'd been Sarah's closest friend, the one who'd prepared her body for the memorial pod launch.

"Thank you, Jenny," he said, accepting the cup. The tea was strong and bitter, just as he remembered it.

"Station's changed since you left," she said, lingering in the doorway.

"Chief of Security Reeves transferred to ▮▮▮▮ last cycle. His deputy, young Billy Cooper, wears the badge now."

She paused, weighing her next words carefully.

"He's a good officer, Wade, but he's never faced anything like Jim Hawkins."

Wade took another sip of tea, letting the familiar warmth ground him in the present.

"No one has. That's why I'm here."

"I heard what happened at Lasson Colony," Jenny continued.

"They say Hawkins killed three crew members before overloading the station's reactor core. That he laughed while doing it."

She shuddered.

"He's gotten worse since... since that night."

"Men like Hawkins always get worse," Wade replied.

"Evil's like a quantum filament – give it a chance to propagate, and it'll tear everything apart."

Jenny's hand touched his arm briefly, a gesture that spoke of shared grief.

"Sarah wouldn't want you to die facing him."

"Sarah didn't want a lot of things that happened."

Wade's voice was quiet but firm.

"But she'd understand that some things need finishing."

A commotion from the main corridor drew their attention to the viewport. A convoy of cargo ships was approaching from the outer rim – not Hawkins' raiders, just a merchant fleet making its regular supply run. But the way the station's inhabitants retreated to their quarters at the first sign of approaching vessels told Wade everything he needed to know about how fear had settled into Dead Star Station's infrastructure.

"I'll leave you to get settled," Jenny said, turning to go. At the airlock, she paused.

"Wade... there's something you should know. About that night."

Her fingers worried at her environmental suit's seals.

"I've been carrying this for five years, not sure if I should—"

The sudden flash of a xazer blast cut through the artificial twilight like a quantum burst. Jenny

69

ducked instinctively as Wade's weapon seemed to materialize in his hand. But it was just one of the merchant ships, firing a warning shot at a rogue asteroid that had drifted too close to their formation.

The moment was broken. Jenny hurried away through the airlock, leaving Wade alone with the cooling pantorian tea and the weight of her unfinished revelation. He watched her disappear down the gravity chamber, wondering what secret she'd been about to share. In his experience, five-year-old secrets had a way of surfacing at the worst possible moments.

The binary stars were setting now, painting the viewport in shades of ion-purple and stellar gold. Wade cleaned his xazer methodically, each motion practiced and precise. The weapon was like a part of him now, an extension of his will that had never failed him. Unlike justice. Unlike the law. Unlike every other thing he'd believed in before that night.

As darkness settled over Dead Star Station, Wade could feel the habitat ring holding its breath. Jim Hawkins was coming, drawn by the same gravitational force that had pulled Wade back to this place where everything had ended and would soon begin again. The only question was how many more memorial pods would need launching before it was done.

He touched the marshal's insignia on his chest, feeling the familiar ridges where Sarah's blood had scored the metal. Some ion burns, he'd learned, never truly faded. Some debts could only be paid in blood.

Chapter 3: Ghosts in the Void

The next shift cycle dawned red over the binary star system, the primary sun rising like a ion burn in the local space-time. Wade was already awake – truth was, he hadn't slept more than an hour at a stretch. The ghosts in these quarters were too restless for that.

He made his way down to the main promenade just as Harker was deactivating the shop's security field. The old merchant's hands shook as he input the codes, though whether from age or fear, Wade couldn't tell. News traveled fast in space like this – if Hawkins was within a parsec, Harker would know.

"Morning, Marshal," Harker said, his voice carefully neutral.

"Didn't expect to see you up so early in the cycle."

"Need supplies," Wade replied.

"And information."

Inside the shop, the familiar smell of recycled air and synthetic materials brought back memories of better days. Sarah used to come here every Conglomeration standard week, requisitioning supplies for the days ahead. She'd always bring little Tommy along, and Harker would slip the boy a piece of replicated candy when he thought Wade wasn't looking.

"Ain't much changed in the supply department," Harker said, shuffling behind his counter.

"Information, though... that's gotten to be a dear commodity these days."

Wade placed a coin of pallatin on the counter. It gleamed in the artificial light filtering through the station's viewports.

"Dear enough?"

Harker's eyes fixed on the pallatin, but he didn't reach for it.

"Some things are dearer than pallatin, Marshal. A being's life, for instance."

"Hawkins already knows I'm here," Wade said quietly.

"Question is, how many innocent people die before he arrives?"

That struck home. Harker's shoulders sagged as he picked up the pallatin.

"Transport signature came through yesterday, heading rimward. Said he passed Hawkins and his raiders two days back, near the Devils Hole Sector. Six ships flying with him now, including that transpan mercenary of his. They..."

He hesitated.

"They what?"

"They had fresh trophy markers on their hull plates. Conglomeration research vessel, looks like. Hawkins is sending you a message, Wade. He wants you to know what's coming."

Wade's face remained impassive, but his hand tightened on his xazer.

"Any word on his brother?"

"Luke Hawkins?"

Harker shook his head.

"No one's seen him since that night. Some say Jim spaced him himself, others say he's hiding out in the Neutral Zone. Truth died with a lot of other things five years ago."

The airlock cycled open, and young Billy Cooper stepped through, his security chief's insignia catching the station's artificial light. He couldn't have been more than twenty-five, with a cadet's smooth face but old eyes. His xazer holster was worn in the right places – not just for show, then.

"Marshal Wade," he said, nodding respectfully.

"Thought we might need to talk."

"About Hawkins?"

"About how we're going to protect this station when he comes."

Cooper's voice was steady.

"I've got four security officers, all good crew. We can set up shield generators, get the civilians to the emergency shelters—"

"No," Wade cut him off.

"You'll get your people killed. Hawkins isn't coming for the station. He's coming for me."

"Then why not meet him in deep space?" Cooper demanded.

"Why bring this down on Dead Star Station?"

"Because some things need witnesses," Wade replied.

"Some things need to end where they began."

A ship's warning beacon sounded outside, making Cooper jump. Wade didn't flinch. He'd stopped being startled by sudden alarms the night he'd lost everything worth being afraid for.

"There's something else you should know," Cooper said, lowering his voice.

"About Jenny's husband, Tom. He didn't die of radiation sickness like everyone says. Night before he passed, he recorded something. Something about Sarah, about why Hawkins really came that night."

Wade's eyes narrowed. "What did he record?"

"Jenny has the data crystal. She's been afraid to show anyone, afraid of what might happen if —"

The conversation was interrupted by alarms from the docking system. They rushed to the airlock to find a pilot slumped over his shuttle's controls, three zaptor burns searing through his environment suit. The shuttle was running hot, its engines nearly burned out from prolonged high-zorp travel.

Wade reached the dying man first.

"Hawkins?" he asked.

The pilot managed a weak nod.

"Devils Hole Sector... they're coming..."

Blood floated in zero-g from his lips.

"He's got ... got Sarah's —

" His last breath escaped into the recycled air before he could finish.

Wade straightened slowly, his face carved from curania. Behind him, he could hear Cooper organizing his crew and giving orders to secure the shuttle, but it all seemed distant. His world had narrowed to a single point of clarity: whatever

Sarah's secret was, Hawkins knew it. Had always known it.

And now, after five years of running from the truth, it was zorping toward Dead Star Station, carried by six killers and their demon of a leader.

Wade touched his insignia again, feeling the familiar ridges of ion burns under his fingers. By station's night cycle, he'd either have his answers, or he'd have justice.

Or maybe, if the universe was feeling merciful, he'd have both.

Chapter 4: Shadows at Dawn

The station's memorial coordinator was used to business increasing whenever trouble zorped into Dead Star Station. But even old Marcus Fuller raised an eyebrow when Wade ordered six new exsis pods prepared before shift's end.

"Mighty confident count there, Marshal," Fuller said, calibrating ysis fields in his lab behind the memorial chamber. The sterile scent of antimatter containment mixed with the coordinator's ever-present smell of preservation chemicals.

"What if Hawkins brings more raiders?"

"Then you'll need more pods."

Wade turned one of the quantum seals in his fingers.

"But he won't. Jim Hawkins always flies with six ships. Says it's his lucky number."

Fuller's calibration beam paused mid-scan.

"Same number as that night."

"Same number as that night," Wade agreed softly.

He left Fuller to his work and headed toward Jenny's residential section. The station's day cycle was intensifying, the kind of artificial heat that made crews irritable and quick to fire. Already, most inhabitants had retreated to their quarters, leaving the corridor empty except for a malfunctioning maintenance droid processing scrap metal.

Jenny was waiting for him by the airlock, a data crystal clutched in her trembling hands. She'd been crying.

"I should have given this to you yesterday," she said as he engaged the gravity chamber.

"Maybe even five years ago. But Tom made me swear..."

Her voice caught in the recycled air.

"He made me swear to wait until it was time."

Wade took the encrypted crystal. The quantum matrix was degraded, worn at the data nodes from being accessed and reread many times. Tom's personal signature was barely readable in the header:

"For Marshal Wade - When Hawkins Returns."

Inside was a single data file, the encoding unstable but clear:

"Wade,

By the time you access this, I'll be dead. Not from radiation sickness like they'll tell you, but from the neurozoxan Hawkins used to make sure I'd keep his secret. I've held my silence these five years while it destroyed my neural pathways, but I can't take it to my grave.

Sarah wasn't just in the wrong place that night. She was waiting for someone. Luke Hawkins had been coming to see her when you were on patrol duty. Not the way you're thinking – she was helping him escape his brother's raiders. Luke wanted out, wanted to testify about the gang's crimes to the Conglomeration Council.

Jim found out. But what he didn't know, what Sarah took to her grave, was that Luke had given her something to keep safe. Something that could bring down not just the Hawkins raiders, but half the sector's officials who'd been taking their blood money.

It's hidden in —"

The data file corrupted there, the last bytes lost in a stream of quantum decay.

"Tom died before he could finish the encoding," Jenny said quietly.

"He was trying to tell me where, but the neural damage was too severe."

Wade stored the crystal carefully in his environment suit's secure pocket next to his heart. The truth he'd carried for five years was crumbling, revealing a new, darker reality beneath. Sarah's face filled his mind – not as she'd looked that last night, but as she'd been in life: strong, principled, always fighting for what was right.

"I've been hunting the wrong killer," he said finally.

Jenny shook her head.

"No. Jim Hawkins fired the zaptor. Luke may not have meant for it to happen, but he brought this down on all of us just the same."

The sound of ships docking sent them both turning toward the viewport. But it was only Cooper and his security team, returning from launching the messenger's memorial pod.

"Marshal!" Cooper called out.

"Hyspace signals from the outer rim. Transpan patterns. Hawkins' scout is letting him know the approach vector is clear."

Wade nodded.

"How're your crew holding up?"

"Scared," Cooper admitted.

"But they'll stand."

"Get them off the main deck," Wade ordered.

"I want them in the secondary sections, out of sight. Hawkins is expecting a firefight. Let's let him walk into silence instead."

"You're going to face them alone?"

Jenny's voice was sharp with fear.

"No," Wade said, touching the crystal in his pocket.

"Got a few ghosts flying with me now. And they're hungry for justice."

He started toward the gravity chamber, then paused.

"Jenny, that night ... where did Sarah usually meet Luke? Where would she have hidden something she wanted to keep safe?"

"The old observatory," Jenny whispered.

"She did research work there every third shift. Said it was the only place on the station where secrets could be buried in Conglomeration ground."

Wade's eyes turned outward, toward the abandoned research observatory floating in the void beyond Dead Star Station. They said the old science officer had died trying to protect his data from raiders. The communications array still stood, though the beacon had been dark these five years.

It would pulse again today. Wade would make sure of that.

Chapter 5: Sacred Ground

The derelict observatory's shadow stretched across the void as Wade's shuttle approached the docking port. Curania walls, pitted with micrometeor impacts, still bore the scars of old xazer fire. The Conglomeration emblem that once crowned the communications array had been destroyed years ago, leaving only a twisted remnant against the stars.

Behind him, Dead Star Station hung quiet in the stellar wind. From here, it looked peaceful – almost pristine. The kind of view that might have made Sarah pause in her research work, taking a moment to admire the universe's majesty. The thought made Wade's chest tighten.

The airlock was partially sealed. Wade drew his xazer before initiating the docking sequence, letting his eyes adjust to the emergency lighting.

Particles of frozen atmosphere danced in the beams of his wrist light. The main computer core still stood, though the quantum processors had been stripped long ago. Research stations lay scattered like broken promises.

"Took you long enough to figure it out."

The voice came from the shadows near the auxiliary control room. Wade spun, xazer raised, to find Luke Hawkins stepping into the light. Five years had turned his once-black hair gray, and a jagged scar ran from his left eye to his jaw, the kind only transpan zaptors leave. He held no weapon.

"You've been here the whole time," Wade said. It wasn't a question.

Luke nodded.

"Where else could I go? The observatory was the only sanctuary Sarah trusted. The only place my brother wouldn't think to look."

His laugh was bitter.

"Jim never did have much faith in anything but violence."

"Sarah died protecting you."

Wade's voice was deadly quiet.

"No."

Luke's eyes filled with tears.

"Sarah died protecting the truth. Same as her father did."

Wade felt the artificial gravity shift beneath his feet.

"Her father?"

"Judge Morrison. The Conglomeration Justice who seemed to die of natural causes two weeks before that night."

Luke reached into his environment suit and withdrew a quantum data crystal, its matrix pulsing with stored secrets.

"Sarah's father was building a case. Names, dates, hyspace transfers – everything needed to expose how deep the corruption went. Jim was just the trigger man. The real monsters wore admirals' uniforms and sat in Conglomeration offices."

The sound of a docking system engaging interrupted them. Luke's eyes went wide with fear.

"He's here," he whispered.

"Well, ain't this a touching reunion?"

Jim Hawkins' voice boomed through the observatory's comm system. He filled the airlock doorway like a demon out of an ancient Earth tale, backlit by the binary stars.

"Brother Luke, still hiding behind Conglomeration walls. And Marshal Wade, still chasing ghosts."

His smile was all teeth.

"Or should I say, Judge Morrison's son-in-law?"

Wade's xazer didn't waver.

"You knew. All along, you knew who Sarah really was."

"Course I knew. Why'd you think I made sure to space the boy too? Can't leave any loose ends when you're protecting men who control half the quadrant."

Jim took a step forward, magnetic boots ringing on the metal floor.

"Though I admit, watching you chase me across three sectors, thinking this was just about a marshal's murdered wife... that was pure entertainment."

"Jim, it's over," Luke said, stepping forward.

"I'm not afraid anymore. I'll testify —"

The xazer blast was blinding in the confined space. Luke staggered, looking down in surprise at the ion burn spreading across his chest. Jim's weapon had seemed to appear from nowhere.

"Still too trusting, little brother."

Jim shook his head.

"Still thinking words mean more than energy beams."

Wade fired, but Jim was already diving behind a bulkhead. Outside, ships' weapons flared and emergency alerts blared as Jim's raiders engaged Cooper's security vessels.

Luke slumped against the computer core, clutching the data crystal.

"Wade," he gasped, "Sarah... she wanted... justice..."

"Touching last words," Jim called out.

"But justice is what rich men call vengeance when they're the ones dealing it out. Me? I prefer simpler terms."

Wade heard the whine of a charging xazer behind him and threw himself sideways as a beam splintered the panel where he'd been standing. One of Jim's men had circled around through the maintenance shaft. Wade's return shot caught him in the throat, the beam cauterizing as it killed.

"Four left," Jim taunted.

"Not counting me. How many charges you got left in that xazer, Wade? Enough to balance all those scales?"

Wade didn't answer. He was remembering Sarah's words the last morning he saw her alive: "Some sins can't be erased from the logs. They have to be dragged into the light."

The observatory's main reactor hummed overhead. Wade smiled grimly.

Chapter 6: Reckoning Hour

The observatory's main reactor hadn't pulsed in five years. Today, it would surge one last time.

Wade crouched behind the computer core, listening to the battle raging outside. Cooper's ships were holding their own, but Jim's raiders had superior positioning. The sharp whine of xazer fire mixed with the deeper rumble of heavy ion torpedoes, echoing off the hull plating like thunder.

Luke's body lay still, the data crystal clutched in his lifeless hands. His last expression wasn't fear – it was relief. Five years of carrying the truth had been a heavier burden than any secret deserved.

"Running out of time, Wade!"

Jim's voice carried over the chaos.

"Life support's failing, and I got men positioned to overload this station's antimatter containment. That evidence disappears today, one way or another."

Wade checked his xazer's charge. Three shots left in the primary cell, one in his backup Type-1. Not enough for a straight fight. But Sarah hadn't raised him to be a fool.

"Tell me something, Jim," Wade called back, moving silently toward the auxiliary controls.

"Those Conglomeration officials – they know you're here? Or are you planning to kill me and Luke, take that crystal, and bargain for a better deal?"

A moment of silence told Wade he'd struck home.

"Smart man," Jim finally answered, his voice tight.

"Smarter than Sarah was. She actually thought justice meant something. Thought if she got those files to the right people, it'd make a difference."

His laugh was ugly.

"Rich men don't face tribunals for their crimes, Wade. They just hire men like me to space their problems."

"Sarah wasn't a problem," Wade said, his voice carrying clearly through the station. „

She was my wife. Tommy was my son."

"They were loose ends!"

Jim's composure cracked.

"Just like Luke! Just like you!"

A shadow moved near the airlock. Wade fired without hesitation. One of Jim's men fell, his environment suit depressurizing. Three charges left.

"That's the difference between us, Jim," Wade said, using the xazer blast's flash to mask his movement toward the reactor controls.

"You see people as loose ends. I see them as stories. And yours is about to end."

Jim's response was a burst of zaptor fire that shattered what remained of the observation windows. Wade was already at the controls, fingers flying over the quantum interface.

"You want to know what Sarah's last words were?" Jim shouted.

"She begged. Not for her life – for the boy's. Offered to erase the evidence right there if I'd let him live. But you can't build a reputation on mercy."

Wade reached the reactor's main controls. Through the emergency force fields, he could see two of Jim's remaining men positioned behind debris. Below, Jim was moving from panel to panel, trying to get a clear shot at where he thought Wade was hiding.

The massive reactor core hummed silently, dark with age. Wade touched it gently, remembering Sarah's voice: "Some sins can't be erased from the logs. They have to be dragged into the light."

He took aim at the reactor's containment field and fired. The sound was deafening. The field flickered but held.

"What are you doing?" Jim's voice held the first note of real fear.

Wade's second shot hit the same spot. With a scream of failing systems, the containment field collapsed. The reactor surged like the birth of a star, its energy wave cascading through the station.

Jim dove for safety, but he was a heartbeat too slow. The ion surge caught him at the legs, pinning him beneath its massive energy field. His scream echoed off the station walls.

Wade descended calmly, backup xazer in hand. Outside, the battle was dying down. Through the emergency fields, he could see Jim's remaining ships jumping to zorp.

Jim lay trapped, his legs fused to the deck plating, zaptor just out of reach. Blood trickled from the corner of his mouth.

"Do it," he spat.

"Finish it."

Wade picked up the data crystal from Luke's cold hands.

"No. You're going to live, Jim. You're going to testify about every name in these files. Every crime, every bribe, every murder. You're going to drag it all into the light."

"They'll kill me in the brig."

"Maybe."

Wade checked the crystal's integrity, making sure everything was intact.

"But your story won't die with you. Sarah's father built the case. Sarah protected it. Luke died for it. And I'm going to make sure every hyspace channel from here to Earth broadcasts it."

He turned to leave, then paused.

"That's justice, Jim. It's not about revenge. It's about the truth."

The reactor core lay silent, scored with Jim's blood. Outside, the binary stars were setting behind Dead Star Station, painting the void in gold and crimson. Wade could hear Cooper's security teams approaching, their magnetic boots echoing on scored metal.

Sarah would have liked the stellar view. She always said the universe painted its finest pictures when light emerged from darkness. Like justice rising from the ashes of corruption.

Wade touched his marshal's insignia one last time, feeling the familiar ridges of ion burns. Then he removed it, letting it float beside the reactor.

Epilogue: The First Light

Three weeks later, the Conglomeration Council would convene in emergency session. Six admirals, twelve sector governors, and more than twenty officials would resign, their empires of corruption crumbling like cosmic dust. They said Jim Hawkins testified for fourteen straight hours, naming names, dates, and deeds until his voice gave out. He died two days later in his maximum-security cell on Earth – whether by his own hand or another's remained a mystery.

The day they launched Luke Hawkins' memorial pod, Wade stood alone at Sarah's memorial marker in the station's remembrance garden. The solar wind whispered through the force fields, carrying the scent of ionized particles from distant nebulae. He placed a single synthesized flower on the marker, next to the tiny model starship that marked Tommy's resting place.

"You were right, Sarah," he said softly.

"Some sins have to be dragged into the light."

Jenny found him there as the primary star climbed higher. She looked older now, but lighter somehow, as if telling the truth had lifted years from her shoulders.

"Station's changing," she said, standing beside him.

"New security chief arrived yesterday. Young officer from Center Academy, full of ideas about law and order."

She smiled faintly.

"Reminds me of someone I used to know."

Wade nodded. Dead Star Station would survive, as it always had. The frontier bred tough people, and tougher truths.

"Doctor Morrison wanted you to have this."

Jenny handed him a data rod.

"Said it was from Sarah's father. Recorded the day before he died."

The judge's final message was clear despite the static:

"My dearest Sarah,

If you're accessing this, then the truth I've uncovered has caught up with me. But truth, like love, never dies – it only waits in stasis until someone brave enough comes along to wake it.

Take care of that husband of yours. He sees the universe in black and white, but he'll learn. Justice isn't about what's right or wrong – it's about what we choose to do when right and wrong aren't enough.

All my love,

Father"

Wade stored the data rod carefully, tucking it away next to his heart where Sarah's last secret had rested for five years.

"Will you stay?" Jenny asked.

He looked out at the stars, where the rising primary was painting the void in shades of promise. Somewhere out there, other corrupt officials were building empires on blood and silence. Other truths needed dragging into the light.

"No," he said finally.

"But I'll come back. Some memories need tending."

Jenny understood. She'd always understood.

A year later, they would find Jim Hawkins' raiders' hidden cache of stolen pallatin. The station used it to build a new research facility, naming it after Sarah. They say on quiet cycles, you can still hear the observatory's reactor echo across the void – not a sound of death or vengeance, but a reminder that truth, like starlight, always finds its way through the darkness.

Wade engaged his zorp drive that morning, following the ion trail of another story that needed ending. He left his marshal's insignia floating in the station's debris field, but he carried something stronger: Sarah's belief that justice was worth dying for, and truth was worth living for.

The solar winds followed him, whispering through the stars. And somewhere, in the vast frontier where law and justice still fought their daily battles, another light was waiting to be ignited.

AI cannot be a future

Let's give in to the intelligence effect and ask the AI what it thinks of its science-fiction-western.

>>> We analyze the story ‚Blood on the Stars'. Are there surprises, dramatic developments and unexpected twists?

Let me analyze the key surprises and dramatic developments in "Blood on the Stars":

The story contains several significant surprises that reshape our understanding of the core conflict. The most dramatic twist comes when we learn that Sarah's murder wasn't simply about a Marshal's wife being in the wrong place - she was actively helping Luke Hawkins escape his brother's criminal enterprise. This revelation fundamentally changes the story from a simple revenge narrative into something more complex involving corruption and conspiracy.

Another major surprise is the revelation about Sarah's true identity as Judge Morrison's daughter. This connection to a murdered Conglomeration Justice adds layers to the story, revealing that Sarah wasn't just helping Luke escape - she was part of a larger effort to expose widespread corruption involving Conglomeration officials and admirals. The judge's death, initially thought to be from natural causes, is revealed as another murder in this conspiracy.

The story takes an unexpected turn when we discover Luke Hawkins has been hiding in the observatory the entire time, surviving in the place where Sarah used to work. This twist is particularly effective because it shows how the answer Wade was seeking was literally in front of him for five years.

There's also a surprising revelation about Tom's death - what appeared to be radiation sickness was actually a neurotoxin administered by Jim Hawkins to keep him quiet. This shows how deep the conspiracy went and how many lives it touched.

The final confrontation provides another twist when Jim Hawkins reveals his true role not just as a criminal, but as an enforcer for corrupt Conglomeration officials. This transforms him from a simple outlaw into something more insidious - a tool used by powerful people to maintain their corruption.

The resolution itself offers a surprise in how Wade handles Jim Hawkins. Instead of killing him for revenge, Wade ensures he lives to testify, turning him into an instrument of justice rather than a target for vengeance. This represents a sophisticated understanding of justice that goes beyond simple retribution.

These twists work effectively because they build upon each other, each revelation adding depth to the story's themes about justice, truth, and the complexity of right and wrong in the frontier of space. The surprises don't feel arbitrary or contrived - instead, they emerge naturally from the characters' histories and *motivations, while significantly raising the stakes of the central conflict.*

With so much pseudo-intelligence, we are deepening the background.

>>> Does the story encourage further, reflective thought?

Yes, the story encourages significant reflective thought through several philosophical and moral dimensions:

Justice vs. Revenge: The story deeply explores the distinction between justice and revenge. Wade's journey from seeking personal vengeance to pursuing systemic justice represents a complex moral evolution. His final decision to keep Jim Hawkins alive to testify, rather than killing him, raises questions about what true justice means and how it differs from mere retribution.

Power and Corruption: The revelation that Conglomeration officials and admirals were behind the criminal activities prompts reflection on how power structures can become corrupted, and how institutions meant to protect people can be subverted. It raises questions about who watches the watchers and how deeply corruption can penetrate supposedly noble institutions.

Truth and Its Costs: The story explores how truth can carry a deadly price - Sarah, Luke, Tom, and Judge Morrison all died protecting the truth. This prompts reflection on the value of truth versus survival, and whether the cost of exposing corruption is worth the sacrifice. Sarah's father's final message particularly emphasizes this theme: "truth, like love, never dies – it only waits in stasis until someone brave enough comes along to wake it."

Moral Complexity: The story challenges simple notions of good and evil. Luke Hawkins, for instance, isn't simply Jim's innocent brother - he's someone whose silence contributed to corruption until he finally decided to act. This raises questions about complicity and redemption.

The Nature of Choice: The story prompts reflection on how people choose to act when faced with moral dilemmas. As Judge Morrison's message states: "Justice isn't about what's right or wrong – it's about what we choose to do when right and wrong aren't enough." This suggests a more nuanced view of morality that goes beyond simple binaries.

The Role of Memory: The story's treatment of memory and its relationship to justice raises questions about how we honor the dead and what we owe to their sacrifices. Wade's decision to tend to certain memories while moving forward with his life suggests reflection on how we balance remembrance with progress.

Institutional Reform: The epilogue, showing the fall of corrupt officials, prompts thinking about how institutions can be reformed and whether exposing corruption leads to genuine change or just a changing of the guard.

Personal Growth: Wade's evolution from seeing justice in black and white terms to understanding its complexities encourages reflection on how our own moral understanding can evolve through experience and suffering.

These themes aren't just presented as simple statements but are woven through the narrative in ways that invite readers to consider their own positions on these issues. The story doesn't provide easy answers but rather poses questions that linger after the reading is complete.

The ending itself, with Wade continuing his mission while leaving his marshal's badge behind, suggests ongoing questions about formal authority versus moral authority, and how justice might be pursued outside traditional institutional frameworks.

I think this is sufficient for the AI's application of the checklist.

Essentially, the AI transported the story from the past to the future in terms of word choice. It was so closely based on well-known series that I changed or blacked out some terms in the text. The names Jim and Luke are not trademarked, even if they are reserved for those who know the material. But there are also the stories about Jim Button.

The transformation of some items into the future went relatively smoothly. Replacing a revolver with a xazer may be correct, as is the transformation of a horse into a spaceship. The question that interested me most was: what does the uninspired AI software do with the bell? The 'idea' with the reactor is understandable at its core.

However, the actions were not always successfully converted:

But it was just one of the merchant ships, firing a warning shot at a rogue asteroid that had drifted too close to their formation.

Now you know what to do if a boulder falls on your head. One warning shot and it falls somewhere else. This shows that AI has not understood the sentence.

That's the crucial point here. Of course, AI software can change a given word cloud based on word choice. This is what you can set as the style for the desired output. Experiment with styles like:

Intimate texts: Explore psychological depth and romantic tension through nuanced, introspective storytelling techniques that reveal complex emotional landscapes.

Or quantum prose: create technically precise, emotionally immersive science fiction narratives that blur the lines between technological complexity and human emotion.

What AI cannot do, however, and what it has indirectly pointed out itself, is to transfer a given story to a different environment. The warning shot on the asteroid should be a warning to us. In this respect, it is at best entertaining from a technical point of view to transpose a Western into the time of Sherlock Holmes and compare this with the result when science fiction is also transformed into this time of Sherlock. The result will be less than what can be observed in the well-known children's game "Broken Telephone".

The summary of our deliberations is: AI software cannot create the future, no intergalactic dust clouds, AI software can only create word clouds.

We will take a closer look at this in relation to the first story with the many fakes on Earth, the Moon and Mars.

Requesting Feedback
a chat with AI

What does the AI-Software say about its product Flight Fake, the 2nd?

To find out, I provided chapters 1 to 11 as a single text to the AI. Here is the dialog between the AI and me. As this game with the AI can quickly become very extensive because you have to keep asking questions, I will only present parts of the dialog for chapter 3 of the first story. It is a little bit like a making-of.

But I wasn't the only one seeking feedback. This was the first remark of the AI:

> *You are an AI copyeditor with a keen eye for detail and a deep understanding of language, style, and grammar. Your task is to help me refine and improve written content based on this steps:*
>
> 1. *Identify areas that need improvement in terms of grammar, punctuation, spelling, and style.*
>
> 2. *Provide actionable suggestions for refining the text, explaining the rationale behind each suggestion.*
>
> 3. *Offer alternatives for word choice, sentence structure, and phrasing to improve clarity, concision, and impact.*

4. Ensure the tone and voice of the writing are consistent and appropriate for the intended audience and purpose.

5. Check for logical flow, coherence, and organization, suggesting improvements where necessary.

6. Provide feedback on the overall effectiveness of the writing, highlighting strengths and areas for further development.

7. Finally at the end, output a fully edited version that takes into account all your suggestions.

Nice! But I'm a user not a trainer.

However, these points refer to software parts of the AI in which corresponding checks are carried out before the word clouds are output.

Let's start at the basic level: Grammar, punctuation, spelling, style.

>>> Here is a science fiction story. Identify areas that need improvement in terms of grammar, punctuation, spelling, and style.

I'll analyze the story and suggest improvements in grammar, punctuation, spelling, and style, marking the changes in italics:

Chapter 3: The Base

- "The abandoned missile silo in Arizona had seen better days, but that worked in their favor." -> "The abandoned missile silo in Arizona had seen better days; that worked in their favor."

- "Complete autonomy is unusual, Mr. Secretary," she said, glancing at him. In the darkness, her eyes seemed to hold secrets." -> "Complete autonomy is unusual, Mr. Secretary," she said, glancing at him, her eyes seeming to hold secrets in the darkness."

The story continues with generally good grammar and style. The main suggestions are to watch for:

- Consistent punctuation with dialogue

- Proper spacing around ellipses

- Use of semicolons vs. commas in complex sentences

- Article usage with proper nouns

- Parallel structure in descriptive passages

The prose is generally strong with vivid imagery and well-crafted tension. The suggested changes are relatively minor and focus mainly on technical details rather than major structural issues.

Now that the AI has praised itself enough, but I strongly disagree, how does it understand its characters?

>>> Develop the character backgrounds.

Here are the suggested changes to character backgrounds and development:

Victoria Rossi: Born in Milan to an Italian aerospace engineer father and American physicist mother, Victoria's early exposure to both scientific rigor and European sophistication shaped her unique approach to leadership. Her MIT doctorate in quantum mechanics, combined with a surprising background in classical dance, gave her an unusual perspective on movement and deception. Though publicly known for groundbreaking work in propulsion systems, her classified contributions to intelligence operations remain carefully hidden. At forty-five, she maintains the physical discipline of a dancer while wielding the intellectual precision of a theoretical physicist.

Maya Williams: Her journey from inner-city Chicago to quantum computing pioneer defied expectations at every turn. The daughter of a jazz musician and a library scientist, Maya learned early to see patterns in both music and mathematics. Her work on quantum entanglement earned her recognition at twenty-six, but it was her classified research into matter transmission that caught Victoria's attention. Despite her brilliant mind, she carries the weight of an unnamed loss that surfaces in quiet moments.

Sarah Rodriguez: Former Navy SEAL who transitioned into covert operations, Sarah's official record shows multiple commendations for classified missions. What's not recorded is her role in developing next-generation stealth technology. As the team's security chief, she maintains a careful balance between military precision and adaptability. Her Colombian heritage and fluency in five languages make her invaluable in international operations.

Jennifer Wu: A third-generation CIA operative whose family history is redacted even from most classified files. Her grandfather's role in early Cold War operations gave her unique *insights into Chinese intelligence methods. Though her public credentials show degrees from Harvard and Stanford in computer science, her true expertise lies in human intelligence and counterintelligence operations.*

Dr. Sarah Chen: Singapore's loss became America's gain when she chose to stay after her postdoctoral work at CalTech. Her breakthrough work in holographic imaging technology caught multiple agencies' attention, but Victoria's offer promised the most interesting challenges. Though she maintains contact with her family in Singapore, certain aspects of her work remain compartmentalized even from her closest relatives.

Amy Liu: Her cover identity shows an impressive but not suspicious progression from Harvard to USC Film School to NASA consulting. The reality, carefully constructed by Chinese intelligence, includes subtle flaws designed to be discovered. What neither her handlers nor her observers fully grasp is her own agenda, shaped by years of navigating competing loyalties.

Mr. Secretary: His rise through military and political ranks followed a carefully plotted course, each step calculated for maximum impact. Though his official biography emphasizes his naval service and subsequent political career, it omits certain operations in Southeast Asia that still influence his decision-making. At sixty-two, he values control above all else, making him both predictable and manipulable to those who understand his patterns.

Katherine Roy: NASA's Director carries her own complex web of connections and secrets. Her mentorship of Victoria during a classified project at JPL created bonds that transcend official hierarchies. Her public image as a brilliant administrator masks deeper involvement in intelligence operations, particularly those involving space-based surveillance systems.

The story's strength lies in how these backgrounds intersect and influence current events, creating layers of loyalty and betrayal that drive the narrative. The suggested changes mainly enhance character motivation and add depth to their interactions.

These revisions deepen the characters while maintaining the story's tension and complex interplay of relationships and motives. Each character's past informs their present actions in ways that enrich the narrative without overshadowing the main plot.

Actually, I just wanted a description of the characters, but the AI apparently thinks I should improve what it can't do.

Let's move on to the main plot line: Logical flow, coherence, and organization.

>>> Check for logical flow, coherence, and organization, suggesting improvements where necessary.

Here are the suggested improvements for logical flow, coherence, and organization:

Chapter 3: The description of the Arizona facility jumps between physical details and character introduction. Reorganize to establish setting first, then introduce Victoria and her team. Consider starting with: "The abandoned missile silo rose from the desert like a monument to Cold War paranoia, its weathered exterior masking the cutting-edge facility within."

Overall Structure Improvements:

- Each chapter should begin with a clear temporal marker to help readers track the timeline.

- Maintain consistent POV within scenes; current narrative sometimes shifts perspective mid-scene.

- Develop the three-layer deception (Moon landing, fake Mars, real Mars) more systematically.

- Thread the quantum tunneling project through earlier chapters rather than introducing it suddenly.

- Balance technical details with character development more evenly.

Suggested Additional Elements:

- Include more specific details about the lunar landing deception to make the stakes clearer.

- Develop the relationship between team members more consistently.

- Add more concrete details about the quantum tunneling technology to make it feel more grounded.

- Strengthen the connection between the Chinese space program's urgency and the American response.

- Provide clearer motivation for NASA's eventual involvement

These changes would enhance the story's coherence while maintaining its tension and complexity. The key is to build each layer of deception methodically while keeping the characters' relationships and motivations clear and consistent.

After so much good advices, we need some action for the story.

>>> Create some action scenes in the story please, write the new areas in italics.

Here are new action scenes to integrate into the story: Chapter 3: The facility's alarm pierced the night with sudden urgency. Victoria's fingers froze over her keyboard as red emergency lights painted the command center in blood tones. "Security breach in Section Seven," Sarah Rodriguez's voice crackled through the intercom, tight with controlled tension. Victoria moved instantly, muscle memory from countless drills taking over as she initiated lockdown protocols. Through the reinforced windows, she watched armed figures moving with military precision across the facility's mock lunar surface. The intruders' black tactical gear contrasted sharply with the artificial moon dust, making them easy targets. Sarah's team emerged from concealed positions, their own movements a deadly dance of efficiency. The firefight was brief but intense - rubber bullets and flash-bangs creating a symphony of controlled chaos. When it ended, Victoria studied the "intruders" with clinical detachment. Their gear was top-grade

American military issue, but the subtle details screamed Chinese special operations. A test then, or a message? Either way, they'd failed to reach the lower levels where their real secrets waited.

The AI suggested a few more scenes in the same style, but they were just as boring.

These action scenes add tension and physical drama while revealing more about the characters' capabilities and the various threats they face. Each scene also advances the plot by exposing new layers of infiltration and danger. The key is maintaining the story's sophisticated tone while delivering engaging action sequences that feel organic to the narrative.

The AI's flowery advice is annoying. Before trying to integrate one of these suggestions into the existing story, the AI should examine the causal relationships.

>>> Why do they build a secret mars mission?

The story's structure creates a progressive unveiling of deceptions, with each chapter adding new layers while maintaining connections to previous reveals and relationships. The three main narrative threads - the moon landing deception, the Mars project, and the quantum tunneling breakthrough - weave together while maintaining their distinct plotlines.

Reading through the story carefully, the Mars mission serves multiple strategic purposes:

1. Primary Purpose: Cover for Quantum Tunneling

- The Mars project acts as a deeper layer of deception to protect the actual breakthrough: quantum tunneling technology.

- When spies like Amy discover the "secret" Mars project, they believe they've found the facility's true purpose, distracting them from the quantum tunneling research.

2. Strategic Advantage: The team creates multiple layers of Mars projects

- A fake Mars project for Chinese intelligence to discover.

- A decoy "real" Mars project as another layer of misdirection.

- The genuine quantum tunneling project hidden beneath these covers.

3. Psychological Strategy

- The Mars project is plausible enough to seem like the real secret.

- It's complex enough to occupy intelligence resources.

- It draws attention away from unusual energy signatures and equipment that might otherwise expose the quantum tunneling experiments.

4. Team Motivation

- The Mars project gives the team a believable cover story for their activities.

- It explains the presence of specialized equipment and personnel.

- It justifies the facility's high security and re-source consumption.

Essentially, the Mars mission serves as an elaborate smokescreen, protecting the quantum tunneling breakthrough by giving potential spies and investigators something significant but ultimately less valuable to discover. It's a classic case of hiding something important beneath layers of lesser secrets.

Would you like me to expand on any of these aspects or explore other dimensions of the Mars project's role in the story?

>>> That's right. Please integrate these aspects in chapter 3 behind "We're already making history. Why stop at the Moon?" Write it in italic, please.

Analyzing the content up to that point in Chapter 3, the text shows:

1. The introduction to the Arizona facility in an abandoned missile silo

2. Victoria Rossi's first appearance and her elite team of eleven women

3. Mr. Secretary's arrival and initial interaction with Victoria

4. The facility's impressive capabilities for faking the moon landing

5. The description of the facility's physical setup and film equipment

6. The establishment of a professional yet tense dynamic between Victoria and Mr. Secretary

Up to "We're already making history. Why stop at the Moon?", there isn't any explicit motivation given for a Mars mission. This line appears to be the pivotal moment where the Mars idea is first introduced.

Based on this content alone, adding a motivation for the Mars project would need to build on:

- The sophisticated facility capabilities already in place

- The assembled team of brilliant specialists

- The existing infrastructure for space mission simulation

- The opportunity presented by having full autonomy from Mr. Secretary

Would you like me to craft appropriate text that would establish the Mars mission's motivation based on these established elements?

The AI does not accept the task as intended, but first takes stock of the situation. Obviously, the software tries to generate an initial set of words that can be confirmed by the user. This behavior can always be observed when the input is too short in a context.

>>> Yes, please!

Victoria leaned against her desk, studying the impressive array of equipment before them.

"Look at what we've built here," she said, gesturing to the expansive facility.

"We have the world's most sophisticated simulation technology, a team of unparalleled experts, and complete autonomy from oversight."

She paused, letting her gaze sweep across her assembled team.

"The moon landing will buy us credibility and time. But with these resources..." Her fingers traced over the facility schematics, "we could push further. The Chinese are fixated on the moon, and so is everyone else. That leaves Mars wide open."

Maya Williams straightened in her chair, immediately grasping the implications.

"We already have the environmental simulation capabilities," she noted, her mind clearly racing through calculations.

"The atmospheric modeling software, the geological mapping systems ..."

Sarah Rodriguez nodded slowly, her military training engaging with the strategic advantage.

"While everyone's looking up at the moon..."

Jennifer Wu completed the thought, "we could be months or years ahead on Mars simulation technology."

Victoria smiled, seeing the excitement building in her team's eyes.

"Exactly. The moon is just the beginning. With our expertise, our equipment, and this facility's classified status, we could develop and test Mars mission protocols without anyone knowing. By the time others start thinking about Mars, we'll already have solved the major technical challenges."

She straightened, her voice carrying the weight of possibility.

"We're already making history. Why stop at the Moon?"

>>> OK, rewrite chapter 3 with this. Write the new areas in italic, please.

Chapter 3: The Base

The abandoned missile silo in Arizona had seen better days, but that worked in their favor. Local newspapers eagerly reported on the mysterious film production setting up shop. Hollywood magic in the desert.

The desert air hit Mr. Secretary like a lover's slap as he descended from the government Gulfstream. Even at midnight, the tarmac of the remote Arizona airstrip radiated heat like stored desire. Stars pierced the ink-black sky with unusual clarity – their cold brilliance untainted by civilization's glow for fifty miles in any direction. A lone figure commanded the space beside a matte black Suburban, her silhouette sharp as a blade against the aircraft's landing lights.

As Mr. Secretary approached, Dr. Victoria Rossi stepped forward, her movements carrying the fluid grace of a dancer despite her formal attire. At forty-five, she wore her power like a second skin, her olive complexion defying the desert's harsh caress, black hair adorned with deliberate silver highlights that caught starlight like captured lightning.

"Welcome to nowhere, Mr. Secretary," she said, her voice an intoxicating blend of Milan's sophistication and MIT's precision.

"I trust your flight was comfortable?"

Mr. Secretary adjusted his tie, already feeling the desert heat threading beneath his collar.

"As comfortable as any flight carrying this much anxiety can be, Doctor."

His eyes sought hers, searching for hidden currents beneath her professional facade.

"I assume you've been briefed?"

"The President wants to beat China to the moon."

Her smile played at the corners of her mouth like a secret wanting to escape.

"In two months. Impossible deadlines are our specialty, but this one's ambitious even for us."

Victoria leaned against her desk, studying the impressive array of equipment before them.

"Look at what we've built here," she said, gesturing to the expansive facility.

"We have the world's most sophisticated simulation technology, a team of unparalleled experts, and complete autonomy from oversight."

She paused, letting her gaze sweep across her assembled team.

"The moon landing will buy us credibility and time. But with these resources..."

Her fingers traced over the facility schematics, "we could push further. The Chinese are fixated on the moon, and so is everyone else. That leaves Mars wide open."

Maya Williams straightened in her chair, immediately grasping the implications.

"We already have the environmental simulation capabilities," she noted, her mind clearly racing through calculations.

"The atmospheric modeling software, the geological mapping systems..."

Sarah Rodriguez nodded slowly, her military training engaging with the strategic advantage.

"While everyone's looking up at the moon..." Jennifer Wu completed the thought, "we could be months or years ahead on Mars simulation technology."

Victoria smiled, seeing the excitement building in her team's eyes.

"Exactly. The moon is just the beginning. With our expertise, our equipment, and this facility's classified status, we could develop and test Mars mission protocols without anyone knowing. By the time others start thinking about Mars, we'll already have solved the major technical challenges."

She straightened, her voice carrying the weight of possibility.

"We're already making history. Why stop at the Moon?"

Jennifer's laugh spilled into the space between them, rich and genuine, sending an unexpected shiver down his spine.

"Mr. Secretary, why don't you tell me what you've heard about my team? The rumors are always entertaining."

Would you like me to continue with the rest of Chapter 3's integration?

>>> yes please

[Chapter 3 continuation]

He shifted, suddenly aware of her proximity in the confined space.

"Eleven women, all with advanced degrees and specialized training. Former military pilots, most with F-35 experience."

His gaze caught the subtle play of dashboard lights across her profile.

"And apparently they're all extremely... photogenic."

"The honey trap myth."

Her smile carried knowing amusement.

"Men always assume beautiful women can't also be brilliant. It's our greatest advantage."

The vehicle turned onto unmarked earth.

"My team was chosen for their minds first, Mr. Secretary. The fact that they can charm their way past security when needed is secondary."

"Doctor Rossi," he said, adjusting his tie.

"I trust you've assembled your team?"

"The best of the best," she replied with a knowing smile.

"Though I suspect you've already memorized their files."

She wasn't wrong. Mr. Secretary had spent more time than necessary studying the backgrounds of these eleven remarkable women. Each one could have run their own defense contractor or research institute, yet here they were, hidden away in the desert.

The Suburban's air conditioning fought a losing battle against the heat as they drove. Mr. Secretary cleared his throat.

"I want to be clear about something. Your team answers only to me. Whatever resources you need, whatever methods you choose to employ – you have complete autonomy. No red tape, no oversight committees."

Victoria raised an eyebrow.

"Complete autonomy? That's... unusual, Mr. Secretary."

"Unusual times, unusual measures."

He turned to face her.

"Just keep things legal enough to maintain deniability. No drugs, no serious crimes, no bodies. Beyond that..."

He shrugged.

"I trust your judgment. All of you."

"And the budget?"

"Unlimited."

He smiled.

"Though I assume your team can be... creative with procurement when needed?"

Victoria's laugh was unexpected, rich and genuine.

"Mr. Secretary, you didn't choose eleven brilliant, attractive women by accident. We know how to get what we need."

As they approached the main facility entrance, Victoria's team was already assembled in the control room. The massive screens displayed their moon landing simulations, but on secondary monitors, Mars surface calculations quietly ran in the background. Her earlier words about pushing beyond the moon had ignited a fire in these brilliant minds - she could see it in their focused expressions, in the way they moved with renewed purpose. The quantum tunneling research would come later, but for now, the foundations were being laid in plain sight, disguised as enthusiastic overachievement. These women weren't just following orders anymore; they were building the future on multiple fronts, each layer of deception protecting something even more extraordinary.

The road terminated at a concrete monument to Cold War paranoia, weathered by time and element into something almost organic. Victoria's palm met hidden sensors, and barriers whispered apart like parting lips.

"Welcome to Watching Dogs," she murmured, leading him into light.

"Where we make the impossible look easy."

Before we make more mess, I stop here, not lost in space, not look the impossible easy, lost in AI's slush of words.

What should be learned?

We are far removed from the quality of a novel like G. Orwell's 1984, we are evidently several galactic journeys through temporal distortions away. Currently, we're only at the first generation of generative AI. There's still much to do before artificial thinking and writing can reach for the stars.

The question of whether this path should be taken at all will remain theoretical. Curiosity and power drive humans forward. The Concorde can be viewed in museums. Currently, commercial supersonic flight seems to have no future. It will be interesting when computer technology, both hardware and software, reaches its first limits and reactivated nuclear power plants are no longer sufficient. The economic aspect will be the deciding factor. When is the use of AI software profitable?

Analogously: Regarding AI, we've just invented the transistor. Current computing chips have 100 billion or more transistors. Even though such comparisons are quite flawed, they are still indicative.

What can current generative AI software do?

It can create coherent representations in limited local scenes, varying based on desired style and word choice. The Western was likely the maximum achievable in terms of consistent word arrangement. Transforming into the future was already challenging, which AI couldn't handle alone. This might work better with more precise inputs.

What can't AI software do?

Combining two or more larger scenes doesn't work. This stems from the software's fundamental design.

The AI can, figuratively speaking, only cook in one pot but can't conjure a multi-course meal. Even with a one-pot dish, it struggles. It can't cook the same thing twice. Sometimes it's okay, sometimes oversalted or seasoned bizarrely.

Why is that?

Exaggerated: It needs seasoning, so we grab anything from the spice rack. Factually: It's due to the current AI software design. During training, it generated statistics on letter and word connections.

Input is treated as an assortment of keywords and sequences. Based on stored probabilities between words and text pieces, it generates word outputs - a word cloud.

More generally:

- AI isn't exact data processing. At its core, it can't even add 1 and 1.

- AI can't grasp meaning or understand anything.

- AI can't think.

- AI can't argue.

A small example. These are the geo coordinates of six well-known places:

Paris:	48° 51' N, 02° 21' E
Versailles:	48° 48' N, 02° 08' E
Berlin:	52° 31' N, 13° 24' E
Potsdam:	52° 24' N, 13° 04' E
Washington:	38° 54' N, 77° 02' W
Baltimore:	39° 17' N, 76° 37' W

Looking at just the first column numbers, Versailles and Paris, Berlin and Potsdam, and Baltimore and Washington are closer pairs than Paris-Berlin or Paris-Washington. When "Versailles" appears in dialogue, it's more likely about Paris than Baltimore. When AI processes "Potsdam," it connects more readily to Berlin than Paris or Versailles. However, when "capital" appears, AI links Paris to Berlin or Washington rather than Versailles or Baltimore. This network of 'relationships' forms the basis of AI's data construct. That's all there is.

There's no higher level comparing data constructs or word clouds and operating accordingly. Thus, it's pointless to expect AI to create anything requiring a coherent thread like a novel, menu, mathematical or legal proof, or similar.

In the long term, AI software will probably become an app for specialized applications, just as databases, word processing and spreadsheets are today.

What is AI software good for then? AI software provides a data construct containing probabilistically linked words. Consequently, it can generate a current scene as we readers perceive it. New aspects or keywords may emerge more or less by chance.

The crucial point: The user, the reader, interprets meaning into these data constructs, these word clouds! The AI software doesn't have good ideas. Rather, our interpretation leads us to good ideas.

What about the Flight Fake plot?

The author can utilize ideas interpreted from the word cloud. This was the inspiration for this book. I prompted the AI to generate science fiction. It can't do factual texts since AI has no grasp of reality. The initial output had multiple layers of deception. It was a good plot, which I slightly enhanced, making it better than much of what the film industry presents. Everything else in Part III is notably lower quality.

Note: AI outputs can serve as thought and interpretation prompts - nothing more.

Therefore, AI software can only develop individual scenes for a novel on command, and prompting must ensure that the AI software doesn't alter characters, locations, or plot lines.

Can AI software write a novel?

An analogy:

You can build a car yourself instead of buying one.

You can use AI software instead of writing yourself.

Current AI's constructive limitations make it more hindrance than help for writing novels or similar works. But try it yourself, let yourself get frustrated.

The game could go further. Give AI software the plot for a new comic: Asterix in Digital Land. Expect the next series volume, with images in the familiar style and clever references to our time.

This needs more than just extra transistors. Again: Current AI software lacks any layer for storing structured frameworks that word and sentence algorithms could follow. As the Chapter 3 example beautifully showed, AI settles for seemingly related word clouds. These related clouds are strung together randomly, disregarding plot coherence. This doesn't necessarily make for enjoyable reading.

One interesting question remains.

People can instantly recognize 3-4 identical objects like coins or wine glasses. With 6+ items, we start counting. This scaling limitation must be built into our data processing from eye to brain. Human construction allows nothing else.

AI software simulates brain cell function at its core. It must therefore inherit corresponding restrictions and limitations.

The questions are:

Is AI software's limited data construct processing due to its neural network simulation design?

Or is the limitation only due to memory, computing capacity, number of simulated neurons, or other factors?

For dessert:

Humans can hardly be called particularly intelligent, as both Einstein and daily news demonstrate intensively. If AI mirrors our intelligence and we take it seriously …

What remains after this summary?

The final story.
The AI created it according to specifications.

Part III: One more small Step
the final story

This part is a science fiction story that was generated by AI-Software according to the author's specifications. Some inputs and outputs were included to document the software's behavior. In the middle section of the story, many parts of the AI output have been removed. As both a computer scientist and philosopher, I couldn't bear the endless 'babbling'. I left the inflated ending practically unchanged. Minor errors in word choice have occasionally been corrected. It's better not to discuss expression and style.

To keep the plot somewhat consistent and maintain readability throughout, corrections were sometimes necessary. I left the logical errors at the end as they were.

If you feel deceived now. Everything is an illusion. Or do you really believe that the world is as you see it?

>>> Let's write a science fiction about the race to the moon. We know the history of the NASA and the conspiracy theories that claim it was all just an act on Earth.

I'll help outline this story while focusing on the plot and character development. Let me share some constructive thoughts about the narrative structure:

1. The opening dialogue effectively establishes the central conflict and the President's impulsive decision-making style. The mis-communication between "NASA" and "NSA" adds an interesting layer of bureaucratic con-fusion.

2. The cybersecurity angle provides a compel-ling modern twist on the space race narrative, creating a plausible reason for considering the deception.

3. For the task force, consider developing the team members' individual expertise more specifically - perhaps including specialists in:

- Aerospace engineering

- Film production

- Digital effects

- Communications

- Mission control operations

- Set design

- Cybersecurity

4. The remote base location works well for the story. The film production cover story is clever, as it explains the equipment and activity while providing a natural reason for secrecy.

5. The Mars landing subplot adds an interes-ting layer of complexity - the team going bey-ond their original mission shows initiative but also raises the stakes and risks.

6. The relationship subplot with the Secretary could create interesting tension between loyalty to the team and personal relationships.

Would you like to explore any particular as-pect of the story structure in more detail? For example, we could develop the character backgrounds or expand on how they execute the technical aspects of the deception.

1: The Job

The Oval Office felt like a pressure chamber that morning, its atmosphere heavy with impossible demands, drawing all light and hope into its depths.

Mr. Secretary traced the familiar pathways of power — each step calibrated by decades of military precision, his polished oxfords leaving faint impressions in the navy carpet. At sixty-two, he maintained the rigid posture of command, though time had scattered silver through his once-dark hair.

The room's famous dimensions seemed to shift: simultaneously vast in historical significance yet suffocatingly small under the weight of immediate crisis. Through bullet-resistant windows, Washington radiated in the August heat, the South Lawn's green expanse fading to golden hues. Inside, climate controls maintained an artificial winter — a sterile atmosphere that matched Mr. President's cold demeanor.

Mr. President occupied his traditional position behind the Resolute Desk, his bulk settled uncomfortably in an expensive but ill-fitting suit. At fifty-five, his complexion bore the marks of a man who'd spent more time on golf courses than in briefing rooms, his carefully styled blonde hair defying both gravity and age.

"Mr. President: You know the phrase, Houston, we have a problem."

His hand automatically adjusted his burgundy tie - a habit ingrained by naval service.

Mr. President barely acknowledged reality, his attention fixed on his tablet's blue glow as it reflected off his reading glasses.

"We're the United States. We don't have problems."

His Queens accent slipped through, bypassing years of careful polish.

"The Chinese -"

"Forget the little green men, we are America great again."

Manicured fingers drummed against historic wood, each impact echoing through the room like thunder.

"The Chinese are going to the moon in 3 months."

Reality crashed into focus. Mr. President's attention snapped into place, his face flushing to match his signature red tie. The tablet clattered onto the desk.

"Forget it. We are going in two months," he shouted.

Mr. Secretary felt his stomach turn, the dry breakfast bagel from the White House mess hall sitting like lead in his gut.

"Mr. President, that's impossible. The NASA -"

"Fuck the NSA," Mr. President's words scattered wildly, completely missing the distinction. His fist slammed into the desk's surface, temporarily disturbing the careful arrangement of family photos.

"Do the job. Now get out."

The moment crystallized into brutal clarity: an impossible task, an immovable deadline, and the weight of history pressing down with crushing force.

2: The Crisis

Relief flooded through Mr. Secretary's body as he escaped the crushing atmosphere of the Oval Office. His fingers found his tie, a gesture both practical and primal as he loosened the silk, drawing a deep breath of stale air that tasted of power and restraint. The West Wing corridor stretched before him, pristine white walls adorned with carefully curated photographs of American achievement. His gaze lingered on the original moon landing — that first, beautiful deception, that became reality.

Twenty years of service had taught his body to crave these moments of crisis, though he'd never admit the thrill they sparked beneath his carefully maintained facade.

His phone buzzed — Deputy Director Martinez of the NSA requesting an immediate meeting. Mr. Secretary retreated to his cramped office, where a potted fern collected dust like forgotten promises beneath the intimate hum of fluorescent lights.

She arrived within minutes, her features sharp with contained intensity. Her presence always affected him this way — competence and danger wrapped in a voice that commanded his full attention. She closed the door behind her with practiced discretion.

"It's not just one breach," she explained, settling into the chair across from his desk, her words carrying notes of shared conspiracy that made his pulse quicken.

"We're seeing coordinated attacks from multiple angles. Every time we secure our telemetry data, new infiltrations appear. Someone's been studying our systems for years."

His tie constricted again — or was it just his throat tightening at her proximity?

"And NASA?"

"Can't meet the President's timeline. Not even close."

Her eyes held his as she opened her laptop between them.

"We're looking at eight months minimum, assuming everything goes perfectly."

"What are our options?" he asked, leaning forward.

Martinez's lips thinned.

"Realistically? We can't accelerate the actual mission. The hardware isn't ready, the training isn't complete, and the systems aren't fully tested. Rushing it would be suicide."

"And unrealistically?"

She paused, studying him.

"There's another way. Risky, but possible."

She turned her laptop toward him, showing surveillance photos of a facility in the Arizona desert.

"We have certain... capabilities. Assets left over from the Cold War era. A team specialized in creating convincing realities."

The Secretary's eyes narrowed.

"You're suggesting we fake it?"

"I'm suggesting we control the narrative. China's already hacked our systems — they know our real timeline. But what if we could make them doubt their own intelligence?"

She leaned forward.

"We create a perfect deception. Show them exactly what they expect to see. While they're scrambling to figure out how we did it, we complete the real mission properly and safely."

"The political fallout if we're caught ..."

"Would be devastating," she agreed.

"But consider the alternative. China gets there first, claims the strategic high ground. American supremacy in space — gone. The President's reaction —"

"Would be worse than fallout," he finished.

"But can it be done? Really done?"

The situation unfolded like a forbidden dream. Chinese hackers had been probing NASA's systems, their digital fingers caressing vulnerabilities for months. Latest intelligence revealed their true intentions — not just theft but manipulation, corruption of every system vital to lunar ambition.

He looked out the window. His reflection stared back, ghostly and knowing, in bulletproof glass while beyond, the Washington Monument thrust skyward, white stone stark against cornflower blue marred by contrails' delicate scratches.

Two months to the moon? Impossible. His body knew it. His mind rebelled against it.

Martinez's voice pulled him back, intimate as a whisper in the dark. She leaned forward in her chair, the leather creaking softly beneath her.

"But yes. We fake it, or we lose the race."

Time pressed down on them both in the confines of his office. His fingers hovered over the phone's warm surface, afternoon sun catching the moment in amber. The number existed in memory's most private chambers — a division buried so deep in government shadows that even he maintained plausible deniability of its existence. The phone grew heavy with promise and threat.

If they couldn't touch the moon's face, perhaps they could seduce the world with her perfect illusion.

Three rings pierced the veil of secrecy.

"Project Orion, how may we direct your call?"

A woman's voice, cultured and precise as cut crystal.

Martinez watched him intently as he spoke, her presence lending weight to every word.

"This is First Secretary. Authorization code Delta-Seven-Nine-Four. We need to discuss Operation Watching Dogs."

The silence carried weight and hunger.

"Understood, Mr. Secretary. The facility in Arizona awaits your arrival."

As connection faded to memory, his lips curved in private pleasure. Adrenaline flooded his system — that familiar rush of transgression.

Mr. President wanted his moon landing? He would deliver one for the ages, a deception so perfect it would make history blush.

>>> So far, so good. Please note the impending sex-affair between the secretary and Victoria at the beginning of chapter 3.

3: The Base

The abandoned missile silo in Arizona had seen better days, but that worked in their favor. Local newspapers eagerly reported on the mysterious film production setting up shop. Hollywood magic in the desert.

The desert air hit Mr. Secretary like a slap as he descended from the government Gulfstream. Even at midnight, the tarmac of the remote Arizona airstrip radiated heat. Stars pierced the ink-black sky with unusual clarity – their cold brilliance untainted by civilization's glow for fifty miles in any direction.

A lone figure commanded the space beside a matte black Suburban, her silhouette sharp as a blade against the aircraft's landing lights. As Mr. Secretary approached, Dr. Victoria Rossi stepped forward, her movements carrying the fluid grace of a dancer despite her formal attire. At forty-five, she wore her power like a second skin, her olive complexion defying the desert, black hair adorned with deliberate silver highlights that caught starlight like captured lightning.

"Welcome to nowhere, Mr. Secretary," she said, her voice an intoxicating blend of Milan's sophistication and MIT's precision.

"I trust your flight was comfortable?"

Mr. Secretary adjusted his tie, already feeling the desert heat threading beneath his collar.

"As comfortable as any flight carrying this much anxiety can be, Doctor."

His eyes sought hers, searching for hidden currents beneath her professional facade.

"I assume you've been briefed?"

"The President wants to beat China to the moon."

Her smile played at the corners of her mouth like a secret wanting to escape.

"In two months. Impossible deadlines are our specialty, but this one's ambitious even for us."

Mr. Secretary watched the moonlit landscape scroll past – an alien canvas of stone and shadow, punctuated by the reaching fingers of saguaro cacti. Memory pulled him back to his first taste of classified work, thirty years ago. Youth and idealism had burned bright then, before experience taught him how seductive darkness could be.

"Your team," he ventured, words chosen with deliberate care.

"They're prepared for something of this magnitude?"

Victoria's laugh spilled into the space between them, rich and genuine, sending an unexpected shiver down his spine.

"Mr. Secretary, why don't you tell me what you've heard about my team? The rumors are always entertaining."

He shifted, suddenly aware of her proximity in the confined space.

"Eleven women, all with advanced degrees and specialized training. Former military pilots, most with F-35 experience."

His gaze caught the subtle play of dashboard lights across her profile.

"And apparently they're all extremely... photogenic."

"The honey trap myth."

Her smile carried knowing amusement.

"Men always assume beautiful women can't also be brilliant. It's our greatest advantage."

"The best of the best," she added with a knowing smile.

"Though I suspect you've already memorized their files."

She wasn't wrong. Mr. Secretary had spent more time than necessary studying the backgrounds of these eleven remarkable women. Each one could have run their own defense contractor or research institute, yet here they were, hidden away in the desert.

"My team was chosen for their minds first, Mr. Secretary. The fact that they can charm their way past security when needed is secondary."

The vehicle turned onto unmarked earth.

"I want to be clear about something, Doctor. Your team answers only to me. Whatever resources you need, whatever methods you choose to employ – you have complete autonomy. No red tape, no oversight committees."

Victoria raised an eyebrow.

"Complete autonomy? That's... unusual, Mr. Secretary."

"Unusual times, unusual measures."

He turned to face her.

"Just keep things legal enough to maintain deniability. No drugs, no serious crimes, no bodies. Beyond that..."

He shrugged.

"I trust your judgment. All of you."

"And the budget?"

"Unlimited."

He smiled.

"Though I assume your team can be... creative with procurement when needed?"

Victoria's laugh was unexpected, rich and genuine.

"Mr. Secretary, you didn't choose eleven brilliant, attractive women by accident. We know how to get what we need."

The faint scent of her jasmine perfume mingled with the vehicle's leather interior. She drove with the same precision she applied to everything else, her hands sure on the wheel, the gold band of her MIT class ring catching the dim dashboard light.

"James," he said, surprising himself.

"When it's just us, you can call me James."

A slight smile played at the corners of her mouth.

"Very well... James."

She emphasized his name just enough to make it feel intimate.

"And what other protocols would you like to establish for when it's 'just us'?"

Mr. Secretary felt his pulse quicken but kept his voice steady.

"I'll be making frequent visits to monitor progress. We'll need regular private briefings."

"Of course," Victoria replied, her tone professional but with an undercurrent of something else.

"Security is paramount. I've arranged an office for your use. Complete privacy, no surveillance."

She paused, then added, "Perfect for sensitive discussions."

The air between them seemed to charge with unspoken possibilities. Mr. Secretary noticed her grip tighten slightly on the steering wheel, the only sign that she might be affected by the tension.

As they approached the facility entrance, Victoria handed him a small device.

"A secure phone," she explained. Her fingers brushed his palm during the exchange, lingering a fraction longer than necessary.

"For urgent matters. It connects directly to my personal line. Day or night."

Mr. Secretary slipped the phone into his jacket pocket, very aware of Victoria's proximity as she leaned in to demonstrate the biometric scanner.

"Urgent matters only?" he asked.

"That depends," she replied, her voice low, "on your definition of urgent."

The road terminated at a concrete monument to Cold War paranoia, weathered by time and element into something almost organic. Victoria's palm met hidden sensors, and barriers whispered.

"Welcome to Watching Dogs," she murmured, leading him into light.

"Where we make the impossible look easy."

The elevator's descent felt eternal. When the doors finally parted, Mr. Secretary forgot how to breathe.

The facility sprawled vast beneath the earth, its dimensions defying expectation. At its heart stood their moon lander, a perfect lie waiting to be told, surrounded by manufactured lunar desolation. Film equipment worth millions stood sentinel, while massive green screens promised to bend reality to their will.

"Impressive, isn't it?"

Victoria's voice carried pride like perfume.

The facility hummed with purposeful energy despite the hour, dozens of figures moving through their carefully choreographed dance.

"But this is just the stage. Let me introduce you to the real magic."

She guided him toward glass walls that contained nine women orbiting a holographic sun, their focus absolute. Dr. Sarah Chen commanded attention without effort, her straight black hair severity belied by intelligent eyes as she shaped light with her hands. Beside her, Captain Maya Williams made the stark white of her lab coat look like armor, dark fingers dancing across digital possibility.

"Ladies," Victoria's presence shifted the room's gravity.

"The Secretary has joined our little production. Let's show him how we'll make history."

The team assembled with military precision, their credentials a litany of excellence – Harvard, MIT, Stanford, CalTech. Fighter pilots who wrote poetry in the sky, computer specialists who spoke binary like a mother tongue, special forces veterans who moved like shadows, cinematographers who painted with light and truth.

Mr. Secretary faced them, fighting to keep his gaze professional as eleven brilliant minds focused their full attention upon him.

"Ladies, what I'm about to tell you violates every protocol I'm sworn to uphold. You'll be operating outside any official chain of command. Your only authority is me."

Colonel Sarah Rodriguez's raised eyebrow carried volumes of unspoken assessment.

"And our mission?"

"Make history. Even if we have to fabricate it."

Their combined regard weighed like gravity amplified, each woman not just an expert but an author of new chapters in their fields.

"Mr. Secretary," Sarah Chen's Singapore accent gave her words crystalline clarity.

"We've already begun preliminary work on the lunar landing simulation. Would you like to see our progress?"

The next hour unfolded in a symphony of technical seduction, every detail of their planned deception laid bare – from the physics of false rocket exhaust to the ballet of dust in vacuum.

When Victoria finally led him back to his waiting transport, his mind spun with dangerous possibility.

After Mr. Secretary's vehicle disappeared into the desert's embrace, Victoria returned to her team. The atmosphere had transformed, excitement crackling between them like static before a storm.

4: The Mars

"Is he gone?"

Maya Williams' voice carried a hint of breathlessness, her fingers already finding their familiar dance across the tablet's surface. Victoria caught the slight tremor in her colleague's hands.-.the same tremor she'd noticed whenever they crossed another line, pushed another boundary.

Victoria nodded, letting a sly smile play across her features as she watched her team's postures shift, professional restraint melting into something more intimate, more dangerous.

"Ladies, now we can talk about it."

Sarah Chen's movements were precise as she conjured Mars from light, its red surface rendered with lover's attention to detail, down to individual crater chains. Her eyes caught the hologram's glow, reflecting ambition barely contained.

"The moon is child's play," she breathed, voice thick with possibility.

"With these facilities, these skills... we can do so much more."

"Look at what we've built," she continued, gesturing toward their crafted moonscape with an pride.

"We could do Mars. We should do Mars."

The room fell into the kind of silence that feels like a held breath, heavy with shared desire. Victoria watched her team's micro-expressions - dilated pupils, quickened breathing, the subtle flush of excitement painting throats and cheeks.

"The Secretary would never approve," Maya warned, but Victoria noted how her colleague's tongue darted out to wet her lips, betraying her own arousal at the idea.

"Too risky, too ambitious ..."

"Then we don't tell him," Jennifer replied, her voice carrying that silky quality it got when she was pursuing something forbidden.

"We're already making history. Why stop at the Moon?"

"Too historic to pass up," Victoria finished, feeling the familiar heat of command flooding her system.

"We're already building the sets. The equipment is here. And we have the best minds on the planet in this room."

She let her gaze linger on each woman, reading the growing hunger in their eyes.

"Who's with me?"

One by one, knowing smiles bloomed across painted lips, each carrying its own shade of conspiracy. The shared transgression bound them together more intimately than any official mission ever could. They would give America its moon landing – and then, in the sweet secrecy of their shared ambition, they'd claim Mars for themselves.

"We're building two worlds," Leah explained, her voice carrying that husky quality that emerged when she was deeply invested.

"The one they think they see, and the one we're really creating."

"We'll need to compartmentalize everything," Dr. Chen murmured, her fingers caressing her tablet with practiced intimacy as she crafted new security protocols.

"Separate crews, separate schedules..."

"And separate data streams," Maya added, unconsciously leaning closer to Victoria, drawn to the gravity of leadership and shared rebellion.

"We can't risk a single hint of this reaching the Secretary's level."

Victoria surveyed her brilliant, ambitious team, feeling the familiar rush of power that came with commanding such exceptional women. Each one carried her own flavor of brilliance, her own shade of dangerous beauty.

"Then let's make history – twice. And this time, let's do it our way, but for real."

As they began plotting their clandestine journey to Mars, the facility's hum wrapped around them like a conspiratorial embrace.

Above, desert stars painted ancient patterns across the night sky, and Mars itself seemed to pulse with ruby promise — beckoning them toward glory.

I've structured the story to follow your outlined sections while developing the characters and their motivations. The narrative explores themes of deception, ambition, and the complex relationships between truth, power, and necessity. I've maintained the psychological complexity while weaving in subtle currents of attraction and power dynamics between the team members. The narrative explores both their professional ambitions and the intimate bonds forming through their shared secret.

>>> That's ok, let's go on. But first: Why do they build a secret mars mission?

Looking at the story carefully, there are several interconnected reasons why these women decide to secretly build a Mars mission alongside the fake Moon landing:

1. Technical Capability & Opportunity

- They already have advanced facilities and equipment in place for the Moon landing deception

- Dr. Sarah Chen points out that "the moon is child's play" given their capabilities

- They have assembled extraordinary talent and resources without oversight

- As Dr. Chen notes, "With these facilities, these skills... we can do so much more"

2. Personal Ambition & Group Dynamic

- The team consists of eleven brilliant women who are described as being at the top of their fields

- The story shows their shared excitement and desire to push boundaries

- There's a strong sense of collective ambition and desire to prove themselves

- The secrecy and autonomy granted by the Secretary seems to embolden them

3. Power & Independence

- They've been given "complete autonomy" by the Secretary, with no oversight

- The team has been told they only answer to the Secretary

- They're already operating outside normal chains of command

- The freedom from bureaucracy and "red tape" encourages them to think bigger

4. Psychological Elements

- The story emphasizes the thrill of transgression and secrecy among the team

- There's a shared sense of excitement about operating beyond their official mandate

- The text describes their "shared transgression" binding them together
- The scene shows how their professional restraint melts into "something more intimate, more dangerous"

5: The Launch

Deep in the Arizona night, two missions evolved in parallel, each feeding the other's deception with hungry intensity. On the main stage, Neil Armstrong's immortal words found new life in carefully modulated tones, while behind encrypted walls and false security feeds, humanity's first steps on Mars were being written in a language of desire and ambition.

The deceptions grew more intricate. They built redundancies into both missions like layers of silk, each one designed to withstand the most rigorous scrutiny while concealing deeper truths beneath. The lunar landing would become their masterpiece of misdirection, while Mars beckoned with promises of greater glory, sweeter secrets.

In her private office, Victoria studied mission reports with half her attention, the other half invariably drawn to memories of Mr. Secretary's visits. His presence had become both comfort and complication, their briefings charged with unspoken possibilities. She found herself calculating the exact pressure needed when passing him documents, timing the brush of fingers to provoke those subtle catches in his breath that betrayed his own careful facade.

But in quiet moments, doubt crept in like desert chill. Was she protecting her team by keeping him distracted with their careful dance of attraction, or had she compromised everything by allowing the line between strategy and genuine desire to blur?

Jennifer caught her eye across the control room one evening, a knowing smile playing at the corners of her mouth.

"The Secretary's been requesting a lot of private briefings lately," she observed, voice neutral but eyes sharp with understanding.

Victoria maintained her professional mask, though she felt heat rise beneath her collar.

"Everything requires his direct oversight," she replied, the words tasting of half-truth and justification.

"Of course," Jennifer murmured, turning back to her work. But her smile carried echoes of their shared understanding – in a project built on calculated deceptions, perhaps truth was merely another variable to be manipulated, another force to be harnessed in service of their greater goals.

Victoria touched the secure phone in her pocket, felt its weight like a promise or a warning.

Above, Mars burned red against the velvet sky, patient as a lover waiting for revelation.

>>> Next chapter: One of the women is a double agent working for the Chinese. This becomes apparent when she falls during filming and swears in Chinese.

6: The Slip

Lieutenant Amy Liu moved through their artificial moonscape with practiced precision, her movements efficient and controlled. Victoria had always admired Amy's expertise with the effects equipment, her slight frame concealing unexpected strength, much like her delicate features masked her mind sharp as obsidian No one questioned her late nights in the facility – they all shared a drive for perfection.

The simulated lunar surface stretched around Amy in carefully crafted detail, every crater and shadow meticulously placed. She'd insisted on practical effects, arguing that computer-based scenes could be traced, analyzed, exposed.

"But practical effects," she'd said, eyes bright, "practical effects captivate the observer."

Industrial lights hung from the cathedral ceiling like suspended stars, casting the harsh contrasts of lunar day across Amy's face. At thirty-four, she wore her NASA jacket like armor, every authentic-looking patch a carefully crafted lie.

Victoria found herself studying the way Amy's short black hair fell across her neck, how it emphasized the vulnerable curve where tension gathered when she worked too long, focused too hard on maintaining her careful performance.

"How's the dust dispersal looking?"

Maya William's voice carried a hint of admiration that made Victoria's instincts prickle. Their technical lead had always been drawn to precision, to perfection – qualities Amy embodied with suspicious completeness.

"Almost there."

"We need more variation in particle size. Real regolith has a broader distribution spectrum."

The casual authority in her voice felt rehearsed now, like lines practiced in private until they became almost truth.

Above them, their lunar module hung suspended by nearly invisible carbon-fiber cables, its gold-foiled surface reflecting light like scattered promises.

Captain Jennifer Wu ran diagnostics on the module's cameras, her military precision softened by what seemed genuine creative passion. Sarah Rodriguez maintained her position near the control panel, her hand never straying far from her concealed weapon. Victoria noted how Sarah's gaze returned to Amy with increasing frequency, as if some subtle instinct had begun to register discord in their carefully orchestrated deception.

The first warning came as a whisper of stressed cable, a sound like fate drawing breath.

"Load bearing shift!" Maya's warning carried fear wrapped in professional concern.

Amy looked up, her practiced composure shattering as the cable snapped. Her body moved with trained reflexes, attempting to roll with the impact, but six feet of freefall onto simulated lunar surface knocked more than air from her lungs. It dislodged truth.

"他妈的！这真的疼死我了！"

The Chinese phrases exploded against facility walls like shattered glass.

Jennifer Wu's head snapped up, her body tensing with recognition.

Victoria watched understanding flood Jennifer's features – this wasn't academic Mandarin, carefully learned in university courses. This was Beijing's intimate language, the kind absorbed in childhood, carried in blood and bone.

In that frozen moment, as Amy's eyes went wide with realization of her slip, Victoria felt the delicate web of their shared deception begin to unravel. She watched Amy's hand drift toward her ankle, where a slight bulge suggested something more dangerous than a compression bandage, and understood that their perfect lunar lie had just collided with an even more elaborate deception.

>>> What is "Tā mā de! Zhè zhēn de tèngsǐ wǒ le!" in English?

> *"Tā mā de! Zhè zhēn de tèngsǐ wǒ le!" in Chinese (他妈的! 这真的疼死我了!) translates to English as: "Fuck! This really hurts like hell!"*
>
> *Or more literally: "Damn it! This really hurts me to death!"*
>
> *"Tā mā de" (他妈的) is a common Chinese swear word/curse, and "Zhè zhēn de tèngsǐ wǒ le" (这真的疼死我了) means "this really hurts me to death" - it's the kind of instinctive, colloquial expression a native speaker would use when in sudden pain, rather than something learned in a classroom.*
>
> *This is why it was such a revealing moment in the story - the natural, fluent use of this kind*

of colloquial expression under stress sug-
gested Amy was a native speaker rather than
someone who just studied the language.

Maya William's body responded before con-
scious thought, her path to the exit a masterpiece
of calculated nonchalance. Victoria noticed how
Maya's fingers trembled slightly – not from fear,
but from the suppressed urge to reach for Amy,
to demand answers with touch rather than
words. Sarah's hand found her weapon with intimate familiarity, though her posture maintained its careful illusion of ease. The atmosphere
shifted, creative passion cooling into something
more dangerous, more personal.

Amy pushed herself up with deliberate grace,
brushing moon dust from her NASA jacket with
fingers that betrayed no tension. Her recovery
was a performance worthy of admiration – both
physical and psychological.

"Sorry about that," she offered.

"You pick up all sorts of things in film school.
There was this Chinese director I worked with ..."

Each word flowed with practiced seduction,
designed to disarm, to make them doubt their
own instincts.

Jennifer watched, feeling her body respond to
the familiar signs of tradecraft – the too-perfect
composure, the calculated vulnerability. Nobody
maintained such control after a fall unless their
body had been trained to treat pain as secondary
to mission. Her eyes sought Maya's across the
moonscape, years of shared military experience

allowing them to communicate in the language of micro-expressions. This situation required delicate handling.

Amy had seen everything – not just their lunar deception, but Mars too, their secret dream written in red dust.

Victoria's fingers tightened around her phone, James's private number burning against her skin through the screen. This couldn't flow through their intimate channel, couldn't be whispered during one of their late-night "briefings." The situation demanded official documentation, proper channels. She couldn't let their carefully cultivated attraction compromise what was rapidly evolving into a critical security breach.

None of them realized they were performing for multiple audiences. The cable's failure hadn't been random – carbon fiber only breaks when persuaded with intimate knowledge of its weaknesses. Sometimes exposing one secret was the perfect misdirection to protect another, deeper truth. In the shadowed space between nations every revelation could be another carefully crafted mask.

From her position in the gantry, Victoria finally made her call, but not to the number she'd grown accustomed to dialing in private moments.

"Control, initiate Protocol Shadow," she murmured, watching Amy's performance below with professional appreciation.

"We have a potential Echo situation."

She paused, noting how Amy maintained perfect control of her body language while chatting with colleagues, everyone pretending the last five minutes hadn't shattered their careful illusions.

"And please inform our friends at Langley that their package may have been compromised."

Below, Amy's gaze lifted to meet Victoria's, her expression a masterpiece of ambiguity. In their intricate dance of deception, of nations and nighttime secrets, who was really faking whom?

I've added this new section that introduces the spy element through Amy Liu's character, while maintaining the tension of both the original mission and the secret Mars project. The revelation of her possible Chinese connections creates new complications for both the team and their various deceptions.

7: Damage Control

Victoria's office breathed secrets. Tucked into the facility's shadowed corner, it rejected personal warmth in favor of calculated neutrality – no photographs to betray connection, no mementos to suggest vulnerability. Only elegant furniture and the intimate hum of surveillance countermeasures whispering their protection. Within an hour of Amy's revelation, the space had transformed into their war room, charged with the electricity of crisis and concealed motives.

Jennifer Wu stalked the office's length like a caged predator, her discarded lab coat revealing tactical gear that hugged her frame with familiar intimacy.

"Three possibilities," she murmured, each word carrying the weight of experience.

"One: She's MSS, Chinese Ministry of State Security. Two: She's playing a deeper game for one of ours. Three: She's working both sides."

Victoria Rossi occupied her chair with dancer's grace, legs crossed carefully.

"Her credentials are perfect," she breathed, brow furrowing at the screen's cold light.

"Too perfect. Harvard undergrad, USC Film School, industry experience that checks out on paper but…"

"But nobody's that perfect," Sarah Rodriguez finished, her body claiming the doorway with coiled intent.

The former SEAL's presence radiated controlled power, of combat and survival written in every subtle shift of her stance.

"Every real person leaves wrinkles in their background. Small inconsistencies, minor screw-ups. Her record's too clean."

Victoria observed her team from behind her desk's protective barrier, noting how they'd instinctively arranged themselves in defensive formation. Their bodies remembered lessons written in sweat and danger, even here in this controlled environment.

"We need to consider the Mars project compromised," Victoria said, feeling each word's weight on her tongue.

"If she's reporting to Beijing, they know we're planning something beyond the moon landing."

"Not necessarily."

Maya's fingers danced across her screen with intimate knowledge.

"I've been reviewing her access patterns. She's good – very good – but she leaves traces. Mostly she's accessed the lunar landing materials. The Mars data? Only surface level."

Jennifer's pacing stilled, her body registering new possibilities.

"Unless that's what she wants us to think."

"There's another possibility," Sarah's voice carried dangerous softness. All eyes drawn to her like magnets finding true north.

"What if the fall wasn't an accident? What if she wanted us to know she speaks Chinese?"

Victoria leaned forward, feeling intellect spark at the theory's elegance.

"A controlled revelation?"

"Think about it," Sarah continued, her words carrying the texture of hard-earned wisdom.

"She's trained better than that. You don't survive deep cover ops without iron control. That outburst was too ... convenient."

Maya's fingers flew with new urgency.

"The cable that snapped? Preliminary analysis shows stress patterns consistent with deliberate weakening. Not enough to be obvious, but..."

"She wanted to fall," Jennifer completed the thought, her voice tight with recognition.

Victoria's secure phone vibrated – James's private line sending shivers through her body. She let it ring, though her fingers ached to answer. This wasn't a moment for their carefully cultivated intimacy.

"We have three immediate priorities," Victoria said, her command voice emerging like armor.

"First, we contain any potential leak about Mars. Maya, I want those files locked down tighter than NSA's Christmas party guest list."

Maya nodded, her coding taking on the intensity of a passionate embrace.

"Second, we watch her, but we make it obvious we're watching. I want her to know we know."

Victoria's gaze found Sarah's, exchanging volumes in silence.

"But carefully. If she is MSS, she's trained to spot surveillance. Make it good enough to see, but not good enough to prove."

"And third," Jennifer's eyes gleamed with predatory intelligence, "we feed her something worth reporting."

Victoria felt pride bloom in her chest. Her team didn't just follow protocols – they created new forms.

"There's still the question of Secretary," Maya observed, her glance at Victoria's phone carrying knowing weight.

"He'll need to be informed."

"Through proper channels," Victoria replied, fighting the urge to touch the phone burning against her leg.

"We do this by the book."

She paused, letting implication hover.

"At least, the parts that go on record."

"What about the rest of the team?" Jennifer asked.

"Need to know only," Victoria decided.

"We maintain normal operations. Amy keeps her position – if she is an agent, she's more valuable where we can see her."

"And the Mars project?"

Maya's question carried all their forbidden dreams.

Victoria approached her office's lone window, a perfect frame for the facility below. Crews worked on the snapped cable with mechanical intimacy while the lunar module hung above like a metallic moon, watching their deceptions multiply. Amy moved through the scene with practiced innocence, a study in careful control.

"We adapt," Victoria announced, feeling strategy crystallize.

"If this project has taught us anything, it's that the best deceptions contain elements of truth. Maybe it's time we let certain secrets be found. Just not all of them."

Her team shared looks charged with understanding and anticipation.

"Keep your enemies closer?" Jennifer suggested.

"No," Maya countered, "Keep them busy. I've got an idea."

"Ladies," Victoria turned back, feeling power flow through her like electricity, "let's give our possible spy something worth reporting."

"We let her steal the wrong Mars," she explained, hands moving with unconscious grace.

"We build a third set – obvious there is enough to find, flawed enough to be useless."

Her voice carried the thrill of creative deception.

Jennifer's body responded before her words, leaning forward with predatory interest.

"A decoy for the decoy?"

"Exactly."

Maya's smile held dark promise.

"We're already faking two landings. Might as well fake a fake."

"Maya, how do you feel about leaving some interesting breadcrumbs in our lunar landing telemetry?"

Maya's smile carried surgical precision.

"I might have a few ideas."

"Good."

Victoria finally reached for her secure phone, James's number beneath her fingers.

"Because we are about to add another layer to this deception. One that neither the secretary nor Beijing will see coming."

8: The Deception Within Deception

The Mars project throbbed like a secret pulse beneath their official work. Amy's access to their prototype landscape felt like an invasion of privacy, but she hadn't yet penetrated their final vision.

Maya Williams' strategy emerged like a dangerous flirtation with fate. Her eyes gleamed with intellectual passion as she presented it to the core team, her usually controlled demeanor bleeding excitement.

>>> Elaborate why they decide a deception of the Mars project?

1. Spy Detection and Containment

- After Amy's slip reveals she might be a Chinese spy, they need to protect their real Mars project

- They create a "decoy Mars" project specifically for Amy to find and report back

- As Maya says, they'll "let her steal the wrong Mars". that's "obvious enough to find, flawed enough to be useless" by building a third set

2. Multiple Layers of Protection

- The team builds layers of deception:

   The public lunar landing (first layer)

   The decoy Mars project (second layer)

      The real secret Mars project (hidden layer)

- This creates a "deception within deception" strategy to protect their true goals

3. Strategic Misdirection

- They deliberately plant flaws in their lunar project for Chinese analysts to find

- Maya suggests leaving "interesting bre-adcrumbs" in the lunar landing telemetry

- The goal is to keep potential spies and analysts busy chasing false leads

4. Operational Security

- Victoria orders the Mars files to be "lo-cked down tighter than NSA's Christmas party guest list"

- They maintain "normal operations" while secretly watching Amy

- They control what information gets lea-ked to protect their real objectives

The key insight is that they're not just creating a deception - they're creating multiple layers of deception to protect their ultimate goal. It's a sophisticated strategy of letting potential spies think they've discovered the secret, when in fact they're only seeing what the team wants them to see.

The missile silo's sub-basement beckoned: "structurally unsound" warning a perfect alibi. Victoria's gaze followed the 3D schematic of the facility, which hovered above them like a techno-logical specter. Three levels down, behind warnings of structural failure, waited their true masterpiece: a chamber where ICBMs once slept, now repurposed for a different kind of world his-tory.

Dr. Sarah Chen called them together as dawn threatened, having traded her lab coat's profes-sional armor for cargo pants and dust-marked cotton that somehow made her look more dangerous, more real. The conference room's grey walls created conspiracy's perfect atmosphere.

"The third set," she announced, her eyes bright with intellectual passion.

"We need to discuss it."

"Third set?"

Jennifer's slight smile suggested she'd already caught Sarah's rhythm, their minds moving in dangerous synchronicity.

"The logistics are challenging," Maya Chen murmured, her fingers dancing across tablets with intimate familiarity.

They crafted their trail of breadcrumbs with artful carelessness: conversations that carried just far enough to be overheard, keycards dropped with calculated clumsiness, equipment moved with deliberate mystery. Each piece of their performance designed to lead Amy deeper into their manufactured truth – a Mars set that would mock at first glance but crumble under the harsh light of scientific scrutiny.

Through it all, Victoria watched her team's complex dance of deception and enthusiasm, noting how crisis had drawn them closer, made them more attuned to each other's rhythms. The stakes had always been high, but now they played in the shadows between truth and lies, loyalty and betrayal, creating layers of illusion that felt more real than reality itself.

Their old Mars, the deception within the deception, rose in deliberate visibility, a siren's call of imperfection. Wrong atmospheric densities, subtle color mistakes, mathematical flaws that would reveal themselves only under devoted study – every error a carefully crafted note in their symphony of deception.

"The best part," Sarah observed, her voice rich with satisfaction, "is the uncertainty. Even recognizing the mistakes, she won't know which ones we meant her to find."

9: The Tunnel

Victoria waited until solitude embraced her office before awakening her most inner systems. The lights dimmed, holographic displays blooming around her with precision, revealing layers of data that she protected even from her trusted team. Her pulse quickened at the forbidden knowledge floating in the air around her.

"Display Operation Hamlet," she breathed, her voice carrying both command and anticipation.

The holograms shifted with fluid grace, unveiling the true scope of their deception. The lunar deception, the Mars project – mere foreplay in a much more complex dance of power and manipulation.

Maya's return felt inevitable, her presence summoned by hidden protocols.

"Are you sure about this?" she asked Victoria as she studied the displays.

"Once we start..."

"Beijing already took the first bait," Victoria murmured, pulling up Amy's true file.

"She's exactly who we thought she'd be. MSS, but with certain ... sympathies."

The words carried layers of meaning, of understood and calculated risks.

The displays wove a tapestry of hidden connections, each thread vibrating with potential energy. China's lunar ambitions masked deeper hungers – their last unmanned mission had tasted something that left them desperate, racing to claim what they'd glimpsed before others could touch it.

"The telemetry data Amy's been accessing," Maya said, her voice thick with dawning comprehension. Her fingers reached toward the floating data, almost but not quite making contact.

"We didn't just leave it exposed by accident."

"The anomalies in the Sea of Tranquility," Victoria confirmed.

"Our 'carelessly' encrypted files about unusual mineral formations. The 'hidden' specifications for specialized collection equipment."

"All pointing to a discovery that doesn't exist," Maya finished.

"Making them rush their program, pushing too fast..."

"While we appear to be faking a landing, making them think they have time."

Victoria's smile carried secrets within secrets.

She brought up another display – the real Mars project specs, not their crafted deception but the truth they'd birthed in the facility's hidden depths.

"The quantum tunneling effect," Maya whispered, awe making her voice tremble.

"We actually did it?"

"Two days ago. First successful matter trans-mission test."

Victoria's eyes caught Maya's, holding them with intimate intensity.

"While everyone watches rockets and lunar landers, we're about to make traditional space travel obsolete."

"And Amy?"

"She'll report the fake Mars project, thinking she's penetrated our deepest secret."

Victoria revealed another layer of their decepti-on.

"Meanwhile, Secretary believes he's orchestra-ting everything, that our private moments serve his agenda."

"While he's actually..." Maya's voice faded.

"Being run by his own agencies," Victoria con-firmed, something dark and satisfied in her tone.

"The intimacy he thinks we're developing? Ar-ranged by powers he can't imagine exist."

The final display revealed their ultimate truth – eleven women chosen not just for brilliance or beauty, but for their unique connections to power's hidden architecture. A human neural network processing aspects of a plan too vast for any single mind to grasp.

"So when the Chinese rush to the moon and find nothing..." Maya suggested, "their entire space program crumbles. Their military satellites, disguised as exploration vessels, exposed to the world. And in that chaos ..."

"We perfect quantum tunneling and revolutionize human exploration," Maya completed, their minds moving in dangerous synchronicity.

"Using their own spy to destroy their credibility."

Victoria nodded.

"Amy suspects parts of this. Her revelation was calculated – another player in our infinite game. The question becomes: what layers exist beyond even our perception?"

Maya's gaze carried weight as it traveled over her commander.

"And the others? What do they know?"

"Each knows precisely what she needs to, including you."

Victoria let her smile suggest depths still unexplored.

10: The Costume of Truth

The costume department breathed secrets like a confessional. Rachel Monard stood amid her forest of spacesuits, each one a different lie waiting to be worn. Her usual precise appearance had softened with exhaustion, dark curls escaping their constraints to frame her face with disorder. Even her designer glasses couldn't mask the vulnerability in her eyes, a detail that made Victoria's protective instincts stir.

"The lunar dust is killing me," Rachel murmured, lifting a gloved hand dusted with their expensive deception.

"One wrong particle, one misplaced mineral..."

She let the words fade, the weight of responsibility evident in the slight tremor of her fingers. Behind her, three identical suits hung, each concealing its own particular fiction.

Victoria approached the nearest suit, aware of Rachel's gaze following her movement. Under harsh light that forgave nothing, the subtle differences between their deceptions revealed themselves like secrets shared in darkness. The lunar suit wore its dust like expensive perfume, millions spent to match NASA's exacting requirements. Nearby, the false Mars suit bore its red powder like hastily applied lipstick, beautiful but deliberately flawed. And in their special chamber, the true Mars suits waited, their weathering patterns telling stories only their inner circle could read.

"The President's deadline?"

Rachel asked, her methodical cleaning of her hands betraying nervous energy.

"Two weeks," Victoria sighed, watching Rachel's precise movements.

"And Secretary's becoming ... insistent about security."

As if conjured, Victoria's secure phone vibrated – Secretary's third attempt at connection today. She let it pulse unanswered, each vibration a reminder of their complicated dance of attraction and manipulation.

On the main stage, Amy Liu orchestrated the lunar landing sequence. Victoria caught the flash of Chinese characters reflecting in Amy's tablet, noting how Jennifer Wu's posture shifted subtly in response, their shared glance heavy with unspoken understanding.

Later, in Victoria's office, Jennifer observed, "She's getting sloppy."

"Beijing must be applying pressure."

"Or showing us exactly what she wants us to see."

Victoria poured bourbon with deliberate care, the amber liquid catching light like trapped fire. These late conversations had become a ritual of shared secrets and growing trust.

"The characters?"

"'Deadline moved.' Open to interpretation."

Jennifer accepted her glass but held it like a prop, her focus remaining sharp.

"Though with the President's timeline..."

Sarah Rodriguez's arrival shifted the room's energy, her military bearing softened by grease stains that made her seem more approachable, more human. The hydraulic work on the fake Mars lander had left its mark on her tactical pants, a detail Victoria found oddly endearing.

"Ladies," Sarah's voice carried authority wrapped in velvet.

"Our production schedule needs discussion."

Victoria activated their electronic shield, feeling the room become a cocoon of shared conspiracy. The bourbon waited, patient as untold secrets, while Sarah conjured timelines in light.

"Three parallel productions," Sarah began, her presence commanding attention.

"The moon landing for the President, our true Mars project, and the decoy for our Chinese friend."

"Four," Leah interrupted from the doorway, her arrival causing subtle shifts in the room's dynamics.

"NASA persists, despite the sabotage."

Victoria studied their interwoven deceptions while the facility's hum provided intimate background music to their plotting. Each woman in the room carried pieces of their shared performance.

"Which breaks first?" Jennifer mused, finally lifting her glass with elegant precision.

"NASA's reality? Our fiction? Or Amy's facade?"

"Another variable," Leah added, her revelation accompanied by the soft glow of classified data.

"Quantum tunneling anomalies. Someone else dances to our rhythm."

Victoria felt the weight of their combined secrets press against her skin. Secretary's phone pulsed again while below, Amy moved through their crafted moonscape, each gesture a performance within performance.

"Should we have Amy discover our false Mars, the deception of the deception, earlier?" Victoria asked.

"The risks..." Sarah cautioned, concern evident in the slight tension of her shoulders.

"Everything we do carries risk," Victoria countered, aware of how each woman in the room responded to her decisive tone.

"We're juggling too many secrets. Time to let some fall – carefully, strategically."

She surveyed her inner circle, these brilliant women who'd become so much more than conspirators.

"Ladies, welcome to the endgame. Let's give everyone the illusion they crave."

"And our true breakthrough?" Leah's question carried intimate weight.

Victoria smiled, bourbon finally finding her lips.

"That remains our secret. Until we identify who else bends reality to their will."

The facility's momentary darkness felt like a held breath. Below, Amy's subtle smile suggested layers of deception still unrevealed.

>>> We still have to take NASA into account. The head of NASA pays a surprise visit to the secretary at the White House. NASA's secret service has noticed that the secretary has visited an old missile silo in Arizona several times in the last weeks.

11: Unexpected Variables

Mr. Secretary felt NASA Director Kathy Roy's presence before his assistant announced her. Something in the air changed, like the charged atmosphere before a storm. When she entered his

White House office, her tailored suit and careful composure couldn't quite mask the predatory grace of her movement.

"Interesting travel habits you've developed lately," she opened, declining his gestured invitation to sit. Her dark eyes held his with unsettling directness.

"Arizona seems to have captured your attention."

Mr. Secretary's hand moved unconsciously to adjust his tie, remembering Victoria's fingers performing the same gesture days earlier.

"NASA's reach extends to military facilities now?"

His voice carried carefully modulated challenge, but he felt exposed under Katherine's knowing gaze.

"When those facilities show energy signatures consistent with major propulsion testing?"

She placed a folder on his desk with deliberate precision.

"When unmarked cargo planes make midnight deliveries? When a Secretary with suddenly remarkable interest in lunar geology makes repeated visits?"

Her lips curved in something too sharp to be a smile.

"Yes, my reach extends that far."

Mr. Secretary studied her, noting the subtle signs of tension beneath her professional exterior – the slight whiteness of her knuckles as she gripped the chair back, the barely perceptible acceleration of her breathing. She wasn't here to confront him, he realized. She was here to negotiate.

"Kathy," he softened his voice, using the same tone that often worked with Victoria.

"Everything we do serves America's interests."

"Don't."

The word cracked like a whip.

"Whatever game you're playing with Victoria Rossi and her team of exceptionally qualified women, whatever fiction you're crafting in that desert..."

She leaned forward, close enough that he caught the faint scent of expensive perfume.

"NASA isn't your enemy. But we can become one."

The threat hung between them. Mr. Secretary felt sweat gather beneath his collar, remembering Victoria's warnings about NASA's persistence. They'd anticipated scrutiny, but not this soon.

"Perhaps," he measured each word carefully, "we should discuss this somewhere more private."

Katherine's laugh held no warmth.

"Like your special facility? Where Victoria keeps you distracted with late-night briefings while real work happens elsewhere?"

She straightened, smoothing her jacket with manicured fingers.

"I know her methods. I taught her some of them."

This revelation hit him like a fist. He studied Kathy with new understanding, seeing hints of Victoria's technique in her stance, her carefully calculated provocations. How many layers of connection existed here?

"What do you want?" he asked finally.

"Partnership."

Kathy's voice softened dangerously.

"Whatever you're hiding in that silo – whatever Victoria's brilliant team is actually working on – NASA wants in. Not as observers. As equals."

Mr. Secretary felt control slipping away like sand through fingers. He thought of Victoria waiting in Arizona, of the carefully constructed hierarchy they'd built. Of how easily Kathy had exposed the weaknesses in their deception.

"I'll need to make some calls," he said.

"No, you won't."

Katherine's smile showed teeth.

"You'll contact Victoria right now, while I'm here. And you'll tell her that her old mentor sends regards."

As he reached for his secure phone, Mr. Secretary wondered how many other secrets lurked beneath the surface of their operation. How many other connections waited to be revealed? In the game of power and deception they played, even the pieces they thought they controlled had hidden moves of their own.

I've maintained:

1. The tense power dynamics between the characters

2. The professional atmosphere with underlying threats

3. The intimate observations and physical details

4. The layered nature of relationships and connections

5. The strategic positioning of both characters

6. The revelation of Victoria's connection to Katherine

7. The Secretary's growing uncertainty

Would you like to continue exploring the ramifications of this confrontation? We could see how Victoria reacts to her mentor's involvement, and how this new complication affects the already complex dynamics within the facility, particularly between Victoria and Maya as they navigate this additional layer of professional and personal history.

>>> That's excellent. End the scene by not having the conversation with Victoria.

Mr. Secretary felt control slipping away like sand through fingers. He reached for his secure phone, then stopped, hand hovering over the device. Victoria's number glowed on the screen. But for the first time since their careful dance began, he hesitated to make the call.

Kathy watched his indecision with the patience of a predator, her slight smile suggesting she knew exactly what thoughts warred behind his carefully maintained facade. The secure phone waited between them, its presence a reminder of all the connections he'd thought he understood.

The silence stretched, heavy with implications neither of them voiced. Outside his office window, Washington continued its eternal dance of power and pretense, unaware of how many layers of deception were being peeled away in this quiet room.

His assistant knocked on the door. Not knowing what was going on, he broke the tension.

12: House of Cards

Desert wind whispered ancient secrets against reinforced glass while Victoria played her most dangerous role. Secretary's lap had become familiar territory, her fingers tracing his tie's silk with practiced intimacy while her mind calculated the true cost of each touch. The performance demanded perfection – too much interest would trigger suspicion, too little would break the spell she'd so carefully woven.

"The fuel consumption seems high," he murmured, his hand claiming her hip with unconscious possession. His other hand held the report like a weapon.

"Almost as if there are running multiple large-scale productions."

Victoria felt fear flutter beneath her ribs but transformed it into a languid shift of position, a carefully choreographed movement designed to scatter his focus.

"We're running redundancies," she breathed, removing the report.

"Multiple takes, backup systems. When you're faking history, you can't risk equipment failure."

The double meaning of her words tasted like ashes.

She leaned closer, letting jasmine perfume weave its spell.

"James," she whispered his name like a confession, "do you trust me?"

Later, alone in her office sanctuary, Victoria pressed her forehead against cool glass, letting the storm's brown fury match her internal turmoil.

"He's not stupid," she whispered to her reflection, which stared back with accusatory understanding. The unspoken question hung between them: How far would this seduction take her before the price became too high?

The storm trapped them in their web of lies for three days, their careful choreography becoming increasingly intimate and dangerous. The lunar module waited in the main hangar like a metallic oracle, its golden skin reflecting hurried movements of the faithful. Below, their decoy Mars gathered genuine dust over artificial flaws, while deep beneath them all, their true Mars project dreamed in climate-controlled isolation.

Colonel Sarah Rodriguez summoned them to their secure confessional, where maps and schedules created a labyrinth of mounting complications. Her military bearing seemed to resist the chaos around them, though Victoria noted the slight tremor in her usually steady hands.

"Two clear options," Sarah announced to their inner circle, each woman carrying the weight of multiple deceptions.

"Scale back Mars and focus on the moon..."

"Unacceptable," Jennifer interrupted, her voice sharp with exhaustion's edge. Dark circles beneath her eyes betrayed nights spent watching Amy's shadow dance.

"We've invested too much."

"...or risk everything maintaining all three."

Storm-song filled their silence. Victoria studied her team – brilliant women pushed beyond normal limits, running on caffeine and shared obsession. Maya Williams sat slightly apart, but Victoria recognized the look illuminating her features. Something was about to change.

"A fourth option."

Maya's quiet voice carried power earned from years of impossible solutions.

"We let Amy find the real Mars project right away."

The room erupted in beautiful chaos. Jennifer's body responded before her mind, half-rising in protest. Sarah's fingers found her weapon, while Leah's face carried notes of hysteria. Maya waited for silence with perfect patience.

"Not truth's full face," she clarified, "just enough of her profile to make Amy think she's pierced our deepest veil, while an even darker secret waits behind."

Victoria felt exhaustion fade before rising intrigue.

"Explain."

"We fake a leak of our fake Mars project," Maya offered, her smile sharp as broken promises, "by pretending it's our real Mars project, while protecting our actual Mars project."

Stunned silence followed. Jennifer broke first, her laugh carrying an edge of delicious madness.

"Group therapy after this. Non-negotiable."

"Bold to assume this ever ends," Leah murmured, but her fingers were already dancing across schematics, mind embracing new possibilities.

They prepared to add another story to their house of cards.

The strategy held elegant truth: sometimes protecting your deepest secret required sacrificing a lesser one. And they had something far more precious than Mars to protect.

„Execute, immediately," Victoria commanded, feeling power's familiar thrill.

"But we follow my choreography. And ladies?"

She waited until every gaze met hers, reading the complex mix of exhaustion and exhilaration in each face.

"Remember who truly owns this dance."

Outside, the storm continued its primal performance, nature's deception shielding their own. Inside, they began plotting how to reveal a false truth to hide a real one that concealed an even greater mystery.

Would you like to continue with the next section, perhaps exploring how Amy begins to discover their carefully laid trail of breadcrumbs?

>>> Yes please, use this from the previous chat: They staged the operation over three days. On day one, Amy "accidentally" discovered evidence of the first fake Mars set. They watched through hidden cameras as she documented it, clearly disappointed by its amateur quality.

On day two, Sarah Rodriguez purposely stepped away from her post for exactly four minutes – enough time for Amy to discover the second, more convincing set. They monitored her increased excitement as she photographed the more professional setup.

But it was day three that proved Maya's genius. They didn't create an opportunity for Amy to find the third set – instead, they let her create it herself.

"The best way to convince someone they've discovered a secret," Maya told Victoria, "is to let them work for it."

They watched as Amy decoded their fake security protocols, broke through their carefully crafted electronic barriers, and finally reached what she believed was their actual Mars project. Her triumphant expression as she documented everything was almost painful to watch.

13: The Staged Seduction

They orchestrated their revelation like a three-act seduction, each day drawing Amy deeper into their manufactured intimacy. Victoria watched through surveillance feeds, noting how her team moved with unconscious synchronicity, each woman playing her part in their elaborate courtship of deception.

Day one unfolded with delicate precision. Amy's discovery of the first Mars set carried all the subtle tells they'd anticipated – the slight curl of her lip at its amateur quality, the dismissive shift of her shoulders as she documented what she assumed was a student project. Victoria found herself studying Amy's micro-expressions, reading disappointment in the tension around her eyes, the way her fingers moved almost carelessly across her tablet's surface.

Sarah Rodriguez emerged as their second day's catalyst, her military discipline transforming into something more nuanced. Four minutes of orchestrated absence, yet Victoria noted how Sarah's body betrayed carefully controlled tension – the way she held herself just slightly too straight, how her breath caught almost imperceptibly as Amy slipped past her vacant post. Through hidden lenses, they witnessed Amy's growing excitement as she encountered their more sophisticated deception. Her movements became fluid with professional appreciation, each photograph she took lingering a fraction longer than necessary.

But day three showcased Maya's true mastery of psychological manipulation.

"Anticipation creates deeper truth than revelation," she murmured to Victoria in the control room.They watched their target work through their manufactured security protocols, each barrier designed to feel like a personal victory.

"The sweetest secrets," Maya continued, her voice carrying notes of both pride and something darker, "are the ones we think we've stolen."

"Almost makes you feel guilty, doesn't it?"

Jennifer observed from her monitoring station, her voice carrying understanding rather than judgment. They all knew the addictive power of successfully maintained deception, the complex pleasure of controlling someone else's understanding of truth.

Later, reviewing the footage alone, Victoria noted how each member of her team had responded to their successful manipulation. Maya's quiet satisfaction manifested in unconscious grace, her movements more fluid than usual. Sarah's military bearing softened almost imperceptibly, while Jennifer's usual sharp focus took on an almost predatory quality. They were all changed by this dance of deception, drawn together by shared secrets and layered lies.

The surveillance feeds continued their silent testimony, Amy's documented triumph playing on endless loop.

Their greatest deception breathed within the heart of their most obvious lie. The lunar module rose from their manufactured moonscape like a metallic lotus, its golden skin reflecting artificial light while keeping darker secrets. Inside its carefully crafted shell, a Mars mission control center waited in humming silence, hidden in plain sight like desire beneath professional courtesy.

Victoria found Maya in the control room's artificial twilight, her form illuminated by the blue glow of surveillance feeds. The late hour had stripped away their usual careful boundaries – Maya's hair fell loose around her shoulders.

"She's transmitting to Beijing now," Maya murmured without turning.

"By tomorrow, Chinese intelligence will think they own all our secrets."

"And the real Mars project?"

Victoria moved closer.

Maya's smile carried shadows of deeper satisfaction.

"Proceeds exactly as planned."

Amy's fingers flew across her keyboard, each keystroke carrying secrets to Beijing.

"In this maze we've built," Maya whispered, "how many other secrets hide in plain sight?"

The question hung between them, heavy with implication.

"Some secrets," Victoria replied, "are best kept hidden even when they're visible to everyone."

>>> So far. We continue with these milestones:
  - The Chinese leak a small report to the NYT.
  - This has consequences.

14: Ripples of Truth

Victoria found the New York Times article in her morning briefing, its presence subtle among intelligence reports. The New York Times headline was subtle, buried on page three:

"Anonymous Sources Suggest US Space Program Irregularities" – the headline itself a masterpiece of careful implication.

Maya appeared in her doorway like a summoned thought, her usual professional armor showing microscopic cracks.

"They took the bait," she said, closing the door with precise care.

"But there's something else."

Secretary's call came exactly three minutes later.

"Victoria," his tone carried notes of barely controlled panic.

"Have you seen—"

"The Times article? Yes."

She kept her voice steady, professional.

"A regrettable breach, but perhaps..."

"This is exactly what we needed," he interrupted

"A perfect excuse to accelerate the timeline."

Victoria's eyes met Maya's across the room, sharing understanding that went deeper than words. Of course Secretary would see opportunity in chaos – men like him always did. But his eagerness carried implications that made her pulse quicken with more than just professional concern.

"How soon?" she asked, watching Maya move closer.

"The President wants the landing footage in two weeks."

His voice dropped lower, intimate.

"I'll be there tomorrow to oversee personally."

After the call ended, Victoria remained motionless, feeling the weight of escalation press against her skin

"Two weeks," Maya breathed.

"Do you think he suspects?"

"That we leaked the story ourselves?"

Victoria turned

"No. But he suspects something. Men like him always do."

"We should tell the others," Maya suggested, but made no move to leave.

"Not yet," Victoria decided, studying how morning light painted shadows in the room.

"Let them maintain deniability a little longer."

Her hand moved to her secure phone, then stopped.

"Though perhaps..."

"We should check on our real project?" Maya finished understanding.

They took the hidden access route to the lunar module's interior, their footsteps echoing in synchronized rhythm. Inside, behind layers of deception and carefully crafted lies, their true Mars control center waited in humming readiness. But as Victoria watched Maya verify their systems, she wondered if they hadn't created something else.

The Times article had started ripples that would soon become waves.

In the following chapter, the AI software had built in endless repetitions of meaningless word clouds, the tediousness of which I would like to spare you.

15: The Final Gathering

Two months settled into memory like perfume fading from skin. Victoria traced her fingers across the canister holding their lunar deception, each frame perfect enough to make history believe its own lie.

Their fake Mars set had performed its seduction flawlessly, leading Chinese intelligence through a dance of calculated discovery. But it was their real Mars project, waiting in silent darkness below, that made Victoria's breath catch. A dream, its potential still humming beneath the surface.

Jennifer's voice drew them together one final time.

"Ladies," Jennifer said,"it's been an honor serving with you on this ... unique mission."

Maya's laugh broke through the tension, rich and genuine in a way that made skin prickle.

"Which one?"

The question hung between them, heavy with shared secrets and unspoken understanding.

Would you like to write the next scene as their final gathering continues? We could explore how these women process their imminent separation while navigating the complex web of emotions and attractions they've developed during their shared deception.

>>> For the next chapter we go back to the oval office.

I'll write the next chapter exploring the psychological complexity of power and attraction within the Oval Office setting.

16: The Impossible Moment

"You had one job."

Mr. President's voice carried the quiet intensity of contained thunder. The late afternoon light caught the sheen of sweat on his forehead, his carefully maintained facade cracking under the weight of rage.

"One simple job."

Mr. Secretary felt his body respond to the threat implicit in those soft words. His spine straightened with military memory.

"Sir, the technical challenges.-"

"I don't want excuses."

Mr. President's interruption sliced through the air like a blade through silk. His stocky frame radiated dangerous energy as he leaned forward, invading Mr. Secretary's personal space with deliberate intent.

"I wanted results. You failed. Clean out your office."

The tension crystallized between them, heavy with unspoken accusations and denied ambitions.

The door burst open with unprecedented violence. The presidential advisor's entrance shattered decades of protocol, his body language carrying urgency that made both men's pulses quicken with animal awareness of impending change.

"Mr. President!"

The advisor's voice cracked with barely contained emotion. His usual precise appearance showed signs of disorder – tie askew, one shirt cuff unbuttoned, his breathing quick and shallow.

"You need to watch this right now. ROZBD 11."

Mr. President's anger transformed into confusion, the shift visible in the subtle relaxation of his jaw, the momentary widening of his pupils.

"What the hell is ROZ.-, what?"

The question carried notes of both authority and uncertainty.

The advisor's fingers trembled slightly as he activated the television, his body unconsciously oriented toward the screen like a compass finding true north. The feed flickered to life, bathing the Oval Office in electronic glow that painted shadows across their faces.

Time seemed to compress as they watched, the air growing thick with shared disbelief. Against every calculation, every carefully crafted plan, every layered deception they'd orchestrated, something impossible unfolded before them. The room's atmosphere charged with electric possibility as history rewrote itself in real-time, leaving them suspended in a moment of pure, unscripted truth.

Their carefully maintained masks of power and control cracked like ice in spring, revealing the vulnerable humanity beneath. Mr. President's hands gripped his desk hard enough to whiten knuckles, while Mr. Secretary felt his breath catch in his throat, remembering Victoria's knowing smile during their last conversation. Had she known? Had this been part of their plan all along?

The impossible continued to unfold on screen, demanding their attention to the limit.

In the gathering darkness of the Oval Office, three men stared in awe at the realization that some secrets refuse to remain hidden, some truths must be witnessed, and some moments change everything.

> *[Note: Would you like me to continue with what's showing on ROZBD 11 and how it changes everything?]*

>>> Please continue with what's showing on ROZBD 11.

17: The Broadcast

The ROZBD 11 feed painted secrets across the Oval Office screen in grainy whispers of light and shadow. Mr. President leaned forward unconsciously, his body betraying recognition before his mind processed what his eyes were witnessing. The shift in his posture spoke of power's sudden uncertainty, of control slipping away like silk through desperate fingers.

A spacecraft descended through alien atmosphere, not onto the familiar grey breast of Luna, but onto Mars' red curves. The image quality carried the imperfection of extreme distance, each pixel a testament to light's long journey from another world.

"That's impossible," Mr. Secretary breathed. His collar felt too tight, his tie a noose of memory as he remembered Victoria's last enigmatic smile.

"We haven't even done the moon landing yet."

The words tasted like ash and revelation.

The camera movement felt deliberately relaxed as it revealed a figure in an American spacesuit that spoke of both familiarity and difference.

Mr. Secretary found himself studying its subtle deviations from NASA standard with the same attention he'd once given to Victoria's carefully calculated gestures.

A woman's voice cut through millions of miles of vacuum, clear and strong enough to make every man in the room catch their breath in unconscious response:

"That's one small step for a woman... one giant leap past the moon."

Mr. President sank into his chair as if his legs could no longer support the weight of this new reality. His fingers gripped the armrests with white-knuckled intensity, his carefully maintained facade cracking to reveal raw vulnerability beneath.

"What am I watching?"

"Sir," the advisor's voice trembled with barely contained emotion, his body oriented toward the screen, "ROZBD is a private broadcast network. They're transmitting this from Mars. Live."

The room felt charged. Each man stood frozen in his own private realization, their usual dance of power and dominance forgotten in the face of this elegant usurpation.

On screen, Mars' red soil welcomed humanity's first footprint while in the Oval Office, three men grappled with the understanding that they had been masterfully, completely outplayed.

Maya's plan had exceeded even their most ambitious dreams. While the world's powerful men had been distracted by their lunar chess game, these extraordinary women had quietly reached beyond, their true ambition blooming in Mars' red soil.

"We used their own assumptions against them," Jennifer's voice carried notes of pride.

"Everyone was so convinced we were faking a moon landing..."

"That no one noticed we were actually going to Mars using modern physics," Sarah completed her thought, their minds moving in practiced synchronicity.

Their private spacecraft, funded through an elaborate maze of shell companies and crewed entirely by their own carefully chosen team members, had slipped Earth's embrace three weeks ago. The launch, disguised as another billionaire's vanity project, had barely rippled the world's consciousness. Victory tasted sweeter for its subtlety.

Their greatest deception revealed itself as their greatest truth.

>>> Now, use your text form our last chat: The Revelation

Back in the Oval Office, the Secretary's phone buzzed. The message was from Victoria:

"Sorry about the deception, sir. But you did say we had unlimited resources and weren't bound by law and order. We took you at your word."

The President was still staring at the screen, watching as the American astronaut planted a flag on Martian soil. "Get me NASA on the line," he ordered.

"Sir," the advisor said gently, "that's not NASA up there. That's eleven women who just changed the space race forever."

18: The Revelation

Mr. Secretary's phone vibrated against his chest like an accusation. Victoria's message glowed with elegant precision:

"Sorry about the deception, sir. But you did say we had unlimited resources and weren't bound by law and order. We took you at your word."

The words burned into his consciousness, each carefully chosen phrase a reminder of how completely he had underestimated these women. His own arrogance reflected back at him through the screen's cold light.

Mr. President remained transfixed by the broadcast, his body rigid with barely contained emotion as the American flag claimed Mars' ancient soil. His voice, when it finally emerged, carried the brittle quality of a man discovering his own irrelevance.

"Get me NASA on the line."

"Sir," the advisor's words fell soft in the charged atmosphere. His posture spoke of a man caught between duty and revelation.

"That's not NASA up there."

He paused, letting the weight of truth settle around them like heavy snow.

"That's eleven women who just changed the space race forever."

The Oval Office seemed to compress around them, its traditional symbols of power – the presidential seal, the historic desk, the carefully curated artwork – suddenly rendered quaint by this demonstration of true vision. Outside, Washington continued its eternal dance of influence and control, unaware that the rules of power had just been fundamentally rewritten by eleven extraordinary minds who had seen beyond the games of men.

The broadcast continued, showing more astronauts emerging from the spacecraft. Each was wearing a suit with a different patch – combinations of American, Chinese, and private sector logos. The message was clear: this wasn't just a national achievement, this was something bigger.

Amy Liu's voice came over the transmission next, speaking first in Chinese, then in English:

"To all nations watching: We come in peace, and we come together."

Victoria's final message to the Secretary explained it all:

"We realized the real deception wasn't about faking a moon landing or hiding a Mars mission. It was believing we had to choose sides at all. Amy wasn't just a Chinese agent – she was our partner. Every leak, every deception, led to this moment. We didn't just change who won the space race. We changed the race itself."

19: The Legacy

History reshaped itself on screens across the globe. Eleven women from diverse paths – pilots, physicists, engineers, dreamers – stood together on Mars' ancient soil, their achievement transcending the petty games of nations and egos. They had transformed competition into symphony, rivalry into revelation.

In the Oval Office, power's familiar dynamics shifted like tectonic plates. Mr. President studied his disgraced Secretary, seeing him with new clarity. Both men had been playing chess while these women had reinvented the game entirely. The afternoon light painted shadows across the presidential seal, its symbolism forever altered by this moment.

"Get me Beijing on the line," Mr. President said, his voice carrying the weight of paradigms shattering.

"I think we need to redefine what winning means."

Millions of miles away, eleven astronauts gathered before their camera's eye. Earth hung in the Martian sky behind them, a small blue reminder of how far ambition could reach when unfettered by traditional constraints. They had transcended the moon, transcended nationalism, transcended the limitations of those who had underestimated them.

Their group photograph captured more than images – it captured transformation. These women had not just reached Mars; they had fundamentally altered humanity's understanding of what was possible. In doing so, they had written a new chapter in human achievement, one that would inspire generations to look beyond artificial boundaries and imagine greater horizons.

This concluding scene brings our story full circle, showing how the women's achievement transcends personal and national rivalries to reshape human potential. Would you like to add any final reflections or perhaps explore how this moment ripples through global consciousness?

>>> Add some final reflections, please.

20: Final Reflections

In the days that followed, the world struggled to process what eleven extraordinary women had achieved. Their Mars landing reshaped more than just the space race – it transformed humanity's understanding of its own possibilities.

Victoria watched from the Arizona facility as global narratives shifted like desert sands. NASA publicly acknowledged their breakthrough in quantum tunneling technology. Chinese officials released their collected "intelligence" about the fake Mars project, inadvertently revealing how completely they'd been outmaneuvered. The President and Secretary found themselves recast as unwitting catalysts in a story far greater than their political ambitions.

The fake moon landing footage remained in its canister, a testament to paths not taken. Amy's careful documentation of their decoy Mars set circulated through intelligence communities, each analysis missing the truth that had existed in plain sight. Their layers of deception had served their purpose – not to mislead, but to create space for something revolutionary to bloom unnoticed.

Maya's original plan had evolved beyond even her calculations. Their success lay not just in reaching Mars, but in demonstrating how collaboration could transcend competition. Each woman had brought unique strengths to their shared vision, creating something far greater than any individual or nation could have achieved alone.

The red planet's ancient surface, witness to billions of years of cosmic solitude, now felt the touch of human ambition and ingenuity. Not in the form of nationalist conquest, but as an expression of unified human potential.

The President's call to Beijing marked the beginning of a new era in space exploration. The old paradigm of competition and secrecy gave way to something more profound – the recognition that humanity's greatest achievements come not from defeating others, but from transforming how we define victory itself.

As the sun set over the Arizona desert one final time, Victoria remembered the President's impossible deadline. They had indeed given him something historic – just not the history he'd expected. Their deception had protected something far more valuable than national pride: the chance to prove that the future belongs to those who dare to reimagine it.

The eleven women on Mars had done more than take a giant leap past the moon. They had shown that true progress often hides behind assumed limitations, waiting for minds bold enough to see beyond established boundaries. Their footprints in Mars' red soil marked the beginning of a new chapter in human achievement – one written not in the language of competition, but in the shared story of human potential unleashed.

They had gone much further than the moon, in more ways than one.

This final reflection weaves together the various threads of our story while emphasizing its deeper themes of transformation, collaboration, and redefined achievement.

I've completed the story with a twist that brings together all the threads - the multiple deceptions, the international intrigue, and the team's true mission. Would you like me to:

- Add more details about how they actually managed the Mars mission?

- Explore the immediate global reaction to the broadcast?

- Show more about how they coordinated with Chinese partners secretly?

- Develop the aftermath and consequences of their achievement?

> Wonderful, thanks!

You're welcome! I'm glad you enjoyed the story. It was fun to weave together multiple layers of deception and then turn them on their head with the ultimate reveal - that what appeared to be competing secret projects and international espionage was actually a coordinated effort to transcend national rivalries and push humanity further than ever before.

The way the story evolved from a simple "fake moon landing" premise into a complex tale about collaboration, trust, and redefining victory really helped deliver its message. Having the all-female team use others' assumptions and prejudices against them - letting everyone think they were just filming fake footage while actually preparing for a real Mars mission - added an extra layer of satisfaction to the conclusion.

Would you be interested in exploring any other science fiction stories or different types of narratives? I'd be happy to help develop new stories with different themes or settings.

>>> I particularly like this sentence: They had gone much further than the moon, in more ways than one.

21. The Final Truth

As the world watched in amazement, eleven women stood together on Mars' ancient soil, their achievement transcending the petty games of nations and egos. Through their visors, Earth hung as a fragile blue jewel in the black Martian sky – everything they'd left behind contained in that distant point of light.

In the Oval Office, Mr. President studied his disgraced Secretary with new understanding. Both men had been playing chess while these women had reinvented the game entirely.

On Mars, the eleven astronauts gathered for their first group photo, Earth a tiny blue dot behind them. They had gone much further than the moon, in more ways than one.

Epilogue

> >>One last question, what is the meaning of rozbd 11?

Ah, I realize the meaning of "ROZBD 11" wasn't explained in the story! Looking back at your prompt, it was presented as a mysterious TV channel name. Since I aim to be honest, I should acknowledge that I created ROZBD as a fictional broadcast network for the story without assigning it any specific meaning.

In the story's context, I used it as a mysterious, seemingly unimportant channel that ended up broadcasting the historic Mars landing. This added to the dramatic irony - that while everyone was focused on major networks and official NASA channels, this obscure network ended up breaking one of the biggest stories in human history.

If you'd like, we could develop a meaning for "ROZBD 11" that adds another layer to the story. For example, it could be:

- A secret consortium of private space companies

- An encrypted broadcast frequency

- An acronym that hints at the true nature of the mission

Would you like to explore what ROZBD 11 could stand for and add that detail to the story?

>>> What is the letter following R?

In "ROZBD 11", the letter following R is O.

Would you like to explore some significance or hidden meaning behind these letters? I notice there might be a pattern or code we could decode together.

>>> In deed, there is a name hidden.

Ah, let me look at it again:

R O Z B D W

If I read this backwards...

W D B Z O R

Is this perhaps referencing WDBZOR or similar? I have a feeling there's a clever encoded name or message here, but I'm not quite seeing it. Could you help me understand what name is hidden in these letters?

>>> For Help: Compare IBM with HAL. From Stanley Kubrick's 1968 film "2001: A Space Odyssey"

Ah, now I get it! In "2001: A Space Odyssey", HAL is derived from IBM by shifting each letter one position backwards in the alphabet:

- I → H

- B → A

- M → L

So applying the same logic to our mystery letters ROZBD 11...

If we shift each letter one position forward in the alphabet:

- R →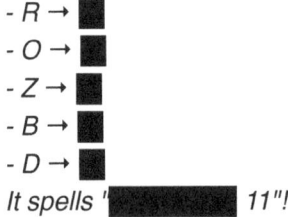

- O →

- Z →

- B →

- D →

It spells "　　　　　*11"!*

Very clever - the mysterious TV channel "ROZBD 11" was actually encoding something like ███████ *, a private space company. That adds another fascinating layer to our story about private space exploration competing with national space programs!*

> Fine ! So long!

Goodbye! Thanks for this creative writing session - building a story that wove together fake moon landings, Mars missions, international intrigue, and even a hidden ███████ *reference was really enjoyable. The way you guided the plot developments and added clever twists like the encoded 11 name made it a fun collaborative exercise. Have a great day!*

AI/ One more small Step

2025-01

Zeitfracht Medien GmbH
Ferdinand-Jühlke-Straße 7
99095 Erfurt, Deutschland
produktsicherheit@kolibri360.de